Learning While Leading

Increasing Your Effectiveness in Ministry

Anita Farber-Robertson

With M.B. Handspicker and Rabbi David Whiman

Foreword by Chris Argyris

An Alban Institute Publication

Library of Congress Card Number 99-69585

ISBN 1-56699-230-3

08   07   06   05   04   WP   2   3   4   5   6   7   8   9   10   11

CONTENTS

FOREWORD

Recently I completed an analysis of advice given by world-renowned executives and consultants on effective action.[1] The advice was full of gaps and inconsistencies. It was flawed. Moreover, the writers were unaware of the flaws. Indeed, they used frameworks and crafted claims in such a way that it would be difficult to discover the flaws. Much of the advice was touted as being actionable. Most of it was not actionable. Where it was, it dealt with routine, nonchallenging problems.

It is refreshing to read *Learning While Leading* because it does not fall into these traps. The advice is not flawed, yet author Anita Farber-Robertson is vigilant in looking for flaws. The advice is not superficial, yet the writer is dedicated to writing a book that is accessible to practitioners. The advice is actionable. If implemented correctly, it will not only produce the predicted results; the results will likely endure.

One inconsistency of the books and articles I reviewed: They claimed that their advice was based not on abstract theory but on actual experience. That claim is false. As you will learn, the human mind cannot produce concrete actions without having a theory. Moreover, the meaning of experience is influenced by the theory that the advice-givers hold, whether they are aware of it or not.

The theory used in this book does not mirror these misconceptions and traps. Indeed, it confronts them head-on, and it does so by using concrete cases that concern important and critical puzzles and challenges in everyday life. For example, you will read that some of the most important barriers to effective leadership are the social virtues most of us are taught in order to act effectively. The ways that the virtues of caring, honesty, concern, and strength are crafted create the foundations for self-sealing, self-defeating action.

Another central problem is this: How do we know what we know? According to the popular literature, the evidence that we know is that we can recite correctly what we know, or that we are able to "walk the talk." In this book you will learn under what conditions and for what problems these claims are true or false. You will also learn that most people are not accurate describers of what they know if the criterion used is to describe accurately how they behave and the impact of their actions. Not surprisingly, their effectiveness tends to be flawed. But surprisingly, they are unaware of the flaws while they are producing them.

All this may sound bewildering and complicated. That is because we use the wrong theories about effective action and develop the skills that, at best, lead to counterproductive consequences. But, we can engage these issues, as Farber-Robertson shows, in ways that solve many of the problems. At the core of the beginning is the theory we use. For example, it appears that human beings hold theories of action that they use to inform their behaviors. Individuals hold theories of action that they espouse. These espoused theories of action vary widely across cultures, age and gender groups, education, wealth, and race.

The problem is that human beings' actions are informed not by their espoused theories but by their theories-in-use. The surprise is that the theories-in-use do not vary. It appears that most human beings have the same theory-in-use. If this claim is true, then we can begin to clear up the bewilderment and the complications. We can make effective action quite manageable.

Another surprise is that the theory-in-use leads to skilled incompetence and to unawareness of skilled incompetence. Thus human beings use skills that are counterproductive to their intentions but are blinded to this possibility. Clearing up skilled unawareness and skilled incompetence can also go a long way toward reducing the bewilderment and the complexity. As you will read, the first problem to be overcome is to reduce the bewilderment that people express about the bewilderment just described.

The book is rich with everyday, nontrivial examples to help readers reconceptualize what is going on, and to develop the skills required to produce effectiveness, especially for issues that are difficult, embarrassing, or threatening. The author not only invents new diagnoses and new solutions. She also produces solutions with actual dialogue that provide the reader with concrete advice whose validity is tested in everyday life and under conditions of everyday challenges.

Learning While Leading is a very good book. It is full of valid advice for people in any context who are interested in increasing their effectiveness as human beings and as leaders.

CHRIS ARGYRIS
Author of *Flawed Advice*
and the Management Trap

PREFACE

I am a confessed institutionalist. I am devoted to the care and preservation of institutions. I love them. And they drive me crazy.

I believe in the value and the essential nature of institutions as instruments for the upbuilding of right human relationships to God and to each other. I stand with Henry Bellows, minister of All Souls Unitarian Church, New York, who said in 1859:

> [E]very radically important relationship of humanity is, and must be, embodied in an external institution. . . .
>
> Would that I could develop here, at a time so forgetful and reckless of the dependence of society on organization, the *doctrine of institutions*, the only instruments, except literature and blood, by which the riches of ages, the experience and wisdom of humanity are handed down *[italics in original]*.[1]

It is not only wisdom that is handed down. The same properties that allow institutions to carry forward what is good into successive generations also allow those institutions to perpetuate error and inflict harm. That's the part that drives me crazy. If uninterrupted, institutions can transmit their errors into perpetuity.

Religious institutions are specifically entrusted with the preservation and conveyance of the most significant and central truths and riches of the human community. It is through our faith communities that we teach our children what is important, what is of value, and how to develop right relationships with God and others. It is in our faith communities that adults attempt to practice those espoused values and relationships.

The way we order ourselves in our churches and synagogues sets the standard for "right order" between people. That is what we mean when we say that ecclesiology is normative polity. The structures of our religious institutions implicitly suggest what is normative for the organization of human relations. When people are discounted or disempowered in the religious setting, the tacit message is that God intended that they be without power or influence. Therefore, errors in religious institutions have particular power to distort relationships and injure people.

Clergy and laity enter into congregational life with powerful longings for healing, for guidance, for spiritual nurture, and for closeness to God. Expectations driven by such deep longings render participants in the community vulnerable, while putting the institution under great pressure to meet high standards and to do no harm.

But religious communities are human institutions. They will err. And like all human institutions, they will often be blind to their errors. When confronted with error, they will more readily behave defensively than seek to learn from their mistakes. And these errors will often have destructive and hurtful consequences for the people. It is not that our faith communities intend to hurt us. It is simply the consequence of their human construction and the inevitability of human sin and error. The nature of the church or synagogue as a place entrusted with the preservation and conveyance of the wisdom of the ages makes it also the unwitting preserver and conveyor of error when the errors go undetected and uncorrected.

Therefore, our task as religious leaders is to help the institution remain faithful to its mission. To the extent possible, we help it to preserve and convey only what is good and true and helpful to the people as they grow in faith. We carry a significant and heavy responsibility. To accomplish that task effectively, we need to know how we can detect errors and learn while leading. We need to guide and teach our faith communities to develop the skills for correction and refinement, so that their beloved church or synagogue will truly teach them and their children how to build right relationships. To the degree that religious leaders lead while learning, engaging in correction and nondefensive detection of error, the community will flourish as it effectively becomes a people of God.

Action science is a model for understanding how it is that institutions and the people who constitute them consistently make errors that go undetected. Developed by Chris Argyris with Donald Schon, the action science model identifies gaps and inconsistencies in the theories that inform professional practice and produce error. The model makes it possible to map professional behavior, diagnose error, and institute correction. These skills are foundational to the discipline of action science.

Action science practitioners have worked with corporations and school systems, with governmental agencies and business consultants. From their findings, they concluded that people consistently "designed" their behavior in ways that prevented learning. These barriers to learning were also embedded in the institutional structures and cultures in which the people lived and worked. When learning is compromised, leaders and the organizations they lead are set up for error, frustration, and sometimes tragic consequences. It doesn't need to be so.

My associates and I have been using the principles and insights of action science for application in religious institutions. We have taught this method to rabbis and priests, ministers and lay leaders. We have worked with people who lead denominations, colleges, nonprofit agencies, congregations, and celibate communities. These leaders brought their puzzles, frustrations, and dilemmas. Stuck and confused, they presented their cases. To their surprise, they became liberated. As they were freed to see what was really going on, and freed to relate in authentic and life-affirming ways, real change and growth became possible for them.

Action science was not developed for religious purposes, but the transformation it engenders and the values it struggles to put into practice have yielded a powerfully effective spiritual tool. Because one key element of this work is to discern the gap between what we espouse and what we practice, it has a particular relevance for religious leaders.

The charge of hypocrisy has been leveled against religious institutions and their leaders since biblical times. The accusation has always been painful to those on the receiving end. We have usually hidden from the truths that evoke those charges. Unable to recognize or acknowledge the log in our own eye, we continue to point out the specks in the eyes of others. From that defensive posture it is unlikely that we can address the gaps that exist between what we preach and what we practice. Action science offers an alternative. It provides the skills that allow us to recognize the truth when our inconsistencies are revealed. More significant, it offers the skills we need to close the gaps and behave more congruently with our proclaimed faith. Incorporating that learning loop into our ministry permits us to make ongoing corrections as we lead. Not only are we more effective as ministers; we are also more present as persons. Those of us who embrace the discipline in our practice of religious leadership are ourselves continually renewed and transformed.

I invite you into this transformative encounter with yourself and your practice. It is an opportunity to experience the sublime in the midst of the ordinary. Through action science the practice of your professional craft can become a personal spiritual practice.

ACKNOWLEDGMENTS

As a first-year master of divinity student I took Meredith (Jerry) Handspicker's class on pastoral care. One afternoon the other students did not understand the concept he was teaching. During the break I went over to him and suggested an alternative way of organizing and presenting the concept that might make it more accessible. He smiled, handed me the chalk, and asked me to teach it, which I did. It was a double gift. He was the first person to encourage me to teach. That made a big difference in my life. More significant, though, was his presence as a nondefensive learner when he occupied the role of teacher. From that simple beginning grew a relationship of mentoring, collegiality, and friendship. As my doctor of ministry advisor, Jerry shared in the enthusiasm of my learning action science and followed closely what transpired as I applied it to congregational and denominational consulting projects. He learned with me. At Andover Newton Theological School, when he and I began teaching the D.Min. seminar based on action science, the man who had been my teacher felt comfortable being my student, as I took the lead. I am grateful to Jerry not only for the encouragement he offered and the confidence he had in me, but for the graceful example of what it means to learn while you lead.

I am grateful to Chris Argyris, who took a chance when, as an unknown doctoral student at a local theological school, I called him at the Harvard Graduate School of Education and asked if I could take his advanced class on action science and research design. I had not taken any of his courses on action science. I was familiar only with his first book, *Theory and Practice: Increasing Professional Effectiveness*,[1] which I had read many times. I wanted to learn how to design my doctoral research so that it would reflect the ethical values his work embraced, while still meeting rigorous research standards. Chris accepted this eager student into his world, and my world opened.

David Whiman, rabbi at Temple Shalom in Newton, Massachusetts, enrolled in the D.Min. seminar several years ago, and we have never been the same. He was highly skilled at asking questions to uncover assumptions and inconsistencies. He took the action science material to heart and began to teach it wherever he went. Eventually he came to team-teach it with me for the D.Min. seminar. David too is one who can slip easily with grace and ease from being a teacher to being a learner. His presence allowed me the opportunity to practice the behavior I had cherished in my earlier teacher, Jerry. I could welcome a student into my work as colleague and as friend.

When my sabbatical appeared on the horizon, the opportunity to write the book for which my students had long been clamoring was unmistakable. Well aware of my vulnerability to blindness in areas of vital importance, I knew it would be ineffective and even foolish to try to write this book alone. I needed my own community of inquiry, trusted and insightful, to help me steer this project through the dangers and the snares. Jerry and David agreed to be that community for this project.

We met for hours discussing the project, trying to determine which insights, tools, and skills from action science and our practice we thought were essential to convey. We also explored the realistic limits imposed by teaching through a book. A book provides a linear mode of communication. We had been accustomed to a case-study seminar, which offered the different mode of experiential learning. Together we narrowed the field the book would cover until it was reduced to manageable proportions.

With Jerry's years of work in the ecumenical world of theological education, and David's position as senior rabbi of a major temple in our community, they provided the lenses I would need to be sure that I was speaking as broadly as possible, while remaining faithful to my own traditions. They helped me recognize when beliefs or positions I held were not obvious and universal. They proofread most of the manuscript, asking questions and giving me support, encouragement, and invaluable feedback all along the way. They have given this work hours of their valuable time. I feel blessed and grateful.

I appreciate Scotty McLennan's willingness to read the first chapters of this book when it was in its formative stage. His honest and specific feedback improved its clarity.

I have had the good fortune of being surrounded by students who have taught me as much as I have taught them. Without them my understanding of action science and the writing of this book would not have been possible.

I have been blessed by three Massachusetts congregations that have allowed me the privilege of serving them: First Parish Unitarian Universalist–Canton, the Unitarian Universalist Church of Greater Lynn, and Zion Baptist Church in Lynn. They have been learners and teachers with me as we sought ways to be faithful together.

I thank my husband, Ed, and my friends who tolerated my time away from them that this book sometimes required. Your graciousness provided an encouragement which I cherished.

CHAPTER 1

Pastoral Puzzles

Meet Rabbi Daniel Levy, senior rabbi of a large suburban congregation. He was asked for help by the temple's sisterhood. The sisterhood, like many women's groups in established congregations, was experiencing a declining and aging membership, an overload of responsibility, and feelings of frustration. Naturally, the women turned to their rabbi for help and support. Naturally, he responded. He suggested programs they might offer to attract younger women. He proposed ways to structure their organization differently so that a broader population of women would be comfortable as members. He identified tasks they could give up or delegate so that they need not feel overburdened. He felt pleased with himself. He had given them help.

The women of the sisterhood were not pleased. They did not take his advice. They told other members of the congregation that the rabbi was unsupportive, unsympathetic, and generally unhelpful. They did not believe the rabbi liked them.

The Case of the Puzzled Rabbi

Rabbi Levy was mystified and hurt. He withdrew. He'd given them his best advice, and they had dismissed it. He'd attended to them, and they had been unappreciative. They kept doing what they'd always done and kept getting what they'd always gotten. Privately he dismissed them as resistant, foolish old women. Publicly he said, "I gave them help, and they wouldn't take it." The members of the sisterhood noted that, and added undermining to their complaints.

This frustrating dance became a familiar, predictable pattern in their relationship. The women would ask for help and support. The rabbi would give them help and support. They wouldn't take it. He would attribute the impasse to resistance on their part; they would attribute it to uncaring on his part; he would attribute insincerity to their request, and they would attribute undermining to his intent.

Mirroring Behavior

When the rabbi later shared this continuing saga with a colleague, he was startled to have the question raised, "What kind of help and support do they want?" In truth, Rabbi Levy didn't know. He hadn't asked. And he was even more startled by the question "If what you were doing wasn't working, if your sharing of advice, suggestions, and perceptions was not getting you anywhere, why did you keep doing it?"

In the course of that conversation Rabbi Levy understood for the first time that the behavior of which he had been so critical in the sisterhood—namely, repetitive actions that were not getting them anywhere and their refusal to try something new—was the very behavior he had adopted as his own. The rabbi and the sisterhood were mirroring each other, entrenched in a pattern that was not working, and holding the other responsible.

"Designed Blindness"

How is it that the rabbi, feeling smugly wiser, if not holier, could perceive the error in the sisterhood's strategy clearly, as he saw the group repeat the same futile, ineffective behaviors again and again—and yet remain completely unaware that he was doing the same thing? Clearly the rabbi knew that in the face of failure, one should create a new response. We know that he knew it. He tried, in exasperation and with little success, to convey to the sisterhood the need to do something different. And we know that the rabbi's behavior was not instinctually programmed by his DNA; *he has designed it.*

Consider this: Awareness of what is knowable (and conversely, unawareness of what is knowable) is behavior. Behavior is *designed*, either consciously or unconsciously. The rabbi remained unaware of what he knew. He designed his behavior, either consciously or unconsciously—and designed it to include unawareness of information that was available and knowable to him. We have uncovered here a phenomenon we call "designed blindness."

Designed blindness is our choice, conscious or otherwise, to be unaware of that which is available to be known to us. It is we who prevent ourselves from knowing. Often our culture colludes in protecting us from seeing what we do not want to know.

The old maxim, "If at first you don't succeed, try, try again," may be comforting, but it is wrong. It creates the sealed, stuck loops of ineffective behavior we just witnessed. The more helpful strategy would be "If at first you don't succeed, try something different."

Pastor Dyer's Staff Meeting

The Rev. Toby Dyer is senior minister at a church with a staff of six full-time employees, and nearly a dozen part-time employees. At a monthly staff meeting that included all the full-time employees, one subject was discussed at the request of the personnel committee. The committee wanted to know if the staff preferred having annual across-the-board raises, as deemed appropriate and as the budget would allow, or if the staff preferred a merit-raise system.

Most of an hour was devoted to that discussion. People voiced concerns about how merit raises out of a limited pool of money could be fairly determined. In that setting, only one person filled the role outlined in each job description. Consequently, there was little basis for just comparison. Some discomforts surfaced about the creation of competition among the staff. Under such a system, each person's raise would diminish the money available for the compensation of others. Then the room became silent. Following what appeared to be the end of the discussion, Dyer identified the issues raised and summarized the outcome: a decision by consensus to recommend an across-the-board system of increases. The minister was designated as head of staff to present this decision to the personnel committee, which she did.

The following spring, as the committee began to redesign its review process, it held private meetings with each staff member and then with the minister. The committee asked the minister for her opinion on the method of allocating raises.

Dyer resisted the pressure to voice her personal opinion. She advocated for what she understood to be the staff's preference. At the close of the conversation the personnel committee chair informed Dyer that the staff members had told him they would prefer merit raises.

At the next staff meeting Dyer raised the issue with the staff. Over the course of conversation, two staff members acknowledged that they had told the personnel committee they would prefer merit raises. Dyer felt betrayed and set up to look foolish. She had valiantly advocated on their behalf for a position they did not hold. She told them so. The staff members defended their right to change their minds. The conversation went round and round, going nowhere.

Dyer had made an evaluation of staff members' behavior. She determined that their actions were professionally inappropriate. She shared that evaluation with the staff. She explained that the appropriate place to present and discuss a change of mind was in the staff meeting, not with the personnel committee.

Dyer advocated for her position and for her negative evaluation of their behavior. But she did not ask questions to test her assumptions. Neither did she invite staff to ask questions of her. Staff members told her to drop the subject and not to "make a big deal" about it. The staff became defensive. One member asked why Dyer was "hitting us over the head with it." The whole conversation made them most uncomfortable. The meeting ended with all feeling frustrated and in some way wronged. Staff members became sullen. They complained to each other and to friends in the congregation that they felt disrespected and unsupported by the very person who was supposed to be their advocate. One of the staff remarked on how "unministerial" she was. Dyer, meanwhile, withdrew into her own protective, defensive posture. She judged them as untrustworthy and lacking in integrity. How could such an open, egalitarian process, designed for consensus and mutual support, degenerate into angry mutual distrust?

Theory-in-Use

After sharing this case with colleagues, Dyer was able to identify a contradiction in her own behavior. Although her espoused theory was to encourage open and free discussion and exchange of ideas, the behavior she exhibited revealed quite a different implicit theory. We call the theory about which we are able to speak, the values and intentions which we identify as driving us, "espoused theory." Espoused theory is what we *say* we do and what we *think* we are doing.

We call the theory that explains the actual behavior we have produced, even though we have not expressed it verbally, "theory-in-use." We would have difficulty identifying and expressing this theory, even when we are exhibiting it. The theory-in-use is descriptive. It maps the private and usually undiscussable reasoning processes that generate our behavior. Even though we cannot articulate the theory, we know it as we know our own names. We experience it as private, personal, even intimate. We learned the basics when we were very young. We carry it so comfortably that we remain unaware of its presence or its power.

Another person may be able to identify our theory-in-use, though, describing it with words that take us through the sequence of our behavior. In effect, keen observers can create a map of the patterns that drive us. When we hear our theory-in-use sequences, we feel the resonance of a routine we have long inhabited and know quite well.

These theories-in-use are our "old stand-bys," routines that are triggered without our awareness or even consent. Particularly when we are under stress, they step into the driver's seat. As if we were on autopilot, these well-known routines take us down roads we have traveled many times before. Suddenly, we find ourselves in a situation we don't like, doing something we had not intended to do, feeling frustrated and wondering how we got there. Often the situation is one that feels incredibly familiar. By removing the blinders we have designed, we can uncover the theories-in-use that are driving our behavior. Sometimes the process results in our feeling exposed and embarrassed. After all, these are theories formed and practiced without ever having been passed through the fire of conscious adult thought or examination. Identifying the theories-in-use that have driven us to ineffectiveness becomes key as we seek to increase our professional effectiveness.

An example: Dyer's theory-in-use was constructed by colleagues who observed what she actually did. They then obtained her confirmation that the theory accorded with her behavior and experience. Her theory-in-use could be charted as follows:

- When an event has meanings/implications which are obvious to me and not to others:
    Assume they do not understand what happened.
    Assume I do.

- Repeat over and over the events of the story.
    Assume that what is obvious to me will become so to them.

- Do not question my understanding or analysis.

- Do not inquire as to their understanding or analysis.

- Assume they have a covert agenda which is undiscussable.
    Experience myself as open, just, and honorable.
    Experience them as closed, unjust, and dishonorable.

- Feel betrayed, hurt, angry, isolated, and trapped.
    Become enraged.

- Publicly distance myself.
    Privately feel incompetent.

- Judge them as untrustworthy, and give up collaboration.

In fact, although Dyer espoused open exchanges of ideas, she behaved in ways that shut them down. She made negative evaluations of people's behavior without inquiring as to each person's meaning or intent. She advocated for her own interpretation of events and discounted that of others. She thus made it impossible to recognize and validate the information she claimed to be seeking (why people did what they did, and why they believed it was right to do so). In retrospect, if this theory-in-use (of which she was unaware) was reflected in her behavior at the initial staff meeting, it is reasonable to assume that there was never an authentic consensus in the first place: It is unlikely that Dyer would have been able to create a safe space in which the full variety of ideas and opinions could be discussed.

What is more likely is that Dyer herself was operating with a covert, undiscussable agenda: reaching consensus. That undiscussable agenda rendered it impossible for the rest of the staff to express and receive acknowledgment of an authentic variety of positions. Opinions were forced to go underground, only to resurface elsewhere.

How could it be that someone so skillful and successful as Dyer had remained blind to the ways in which she had designed a strategy with a built-in error, one guaranteed to produce the kind of hidden agenda she abhorred? Furthermore, how could she have held other people responsible? It happened because of designed blindness.

Jesus warned the people not to worry about the speck in the other's eye until they had attended to the log in their own. Designed blindness is a very old problem.

Sister Gellerd's Intervention

Sister Elizabeth Gellerd, a religious educator, worked in a large parochial school program. She met with a team that was trying to determine what to do about a child who was not progressing at the expected pace. The child's parents were quite concerned.

The school was dealing with financial issues, and any identification of a child's special needs added to the school's budgetary problems—a factor known to all members of the team. Sister Gellerd also worked with this youngster and his family. She was convinced that the child had a serious problem that needed to be identified.

This meeting of colleagues deteriorated into a series of mini-monologues, with the players presenting their positions and advocating for them. Sometimes two or more people spoke at once. No one inquired about other people's perceptions. No one offered feedback conveying that another's viewpoint had been heard. As each argued on a rational, logical level, the emotional tone of the conversation heated up.

Sister Gellerd's awareness of the family's history and of her own personal history allowed her to empathize with the family. She was deeply committed to their well-being. She acted not only as an educator, but as one who had felt God's call in her engagement with them.

However, she shared none of this knowledge. She participated in the escalating debate as one of the many who spoke and did not listen. Her cause was lost, and the child for whom she advocated would suffer.

Hindsight

Pained by a sense of failure and frustration, Sister Gellerd brought the case to a group of colleagues. After the meeting, she reflected on what her own behavior contributed to such an escalating closed cycle. She was able to discern the following theory, of which she had been unaware, but which nevertheless had governed her behavior.

- When I think something is important, withhold it.

- When angry at not being heard because I haven't said what is important to me:
    Blame others for not hearing what I haven't said.
    Hold them responsible for my lack of participation.
    Give up, withdraw politely, and wonder what is wrong with them.

How could a highly trained educator, skilled in helping people learn, and committed to being a life-long learner, allow a theory such as this, which is anti-learning as well as ineffective, to govern her behavior? It happened because of designed blindness.

Understanding Designed Blindness

Designed blindness is a term coined by Chris Argyris and Donald Schon in 1974 in their book *Theory and Practice: Increasing Professional Effectiveness*. When they teamed up, Argyris was professor of education and organizational behavior at Harvard University, and Schon was professor of urban studies and education at Massachusetts Institute of Technology. They were curious about professional effectiveness, how it functioned, and how it might be enhanced. Their work developed into the discipline of action science.

The two scholars were intrigued by the extent to which highly skilled people behave ineffectively in their professional practice. Most often the people they observed were unable to identify the reasons for their ineffectiveness, or to make substantive corrections. Argyris and Schon undertook a broad research project of observation and discovery. They uncovered and described patterns of behavior that appeared to be both ineffective and universal. In Africa and Asia, Europe, North America, and South America, people repeated the patterns identified by Argyris and Schon as those that got the practitioners into trouble. In light of that discovery, they began to map out these predictable and recurring behavior patterns. They included the thinking patterns that generated the behavior. They called this schema "Model I." It was from this project, and from their desire to develop an alternative, that action science was born. The new behavior patterns were designed to produce increased effectiveness by allowing people to discover and correct errors in the midst of their practice. They called this alternative "Model II."

Designed blindness is one of the central features of the universal pattern of ineffectiveness. It is a behavior in which we routinely engage and which gets us into trouble. We have known about this behavior for a long time. When we observe it in others, we call it hypocrisy. But that is a very shallow understanding of what has happened and is itself, in most cases, an illustration of designed blindness. Those who cry "Hypocrite!" have designed their own blindness to the ways in which they too practice behaviors at odds with the ones they profess. We can spot incongruent behavior in others while remaining unaware of our own. Because the unawareness is designed, the possibility of our attaining awareness is always with us. That capacity for both blindness and awareness explains why Jesus could stop the crowd about to stone the woman caught in adultery by simply saying, "Let anyone among you who is without sin be the first to throw a stone at her" (John 8:7).

We leap to judgment of others, without reflecting on ourselves, and we judge others by criteria from which we have excused ourselves. We do not do it intentionally. Neither are we aware of what we do. Yet we do it consistently and predictably. We design blindness when we produce our behaviors and make our judgments. We do not know what others can clearly see—that we judge others negatively for behavior in which we engage ourselves.

Cognitive Dissonance

Why are we so hypocritical? While the gap between the values we espouse and the way we behave can be seen by those with whom we interact, it is something of which we are unaware. Yet the information is available to us. It is knowable. That we *choose* not to know is a mode of self-protection, designed to shield us from the unpleasant and ultimately intolerable experience of cognitive dissonance. We find it impossible to live with the knowledge that we behave in ways we dislike or condemn in others.

One reaction to the experience of cognitive dissonance—one that is maladaptive but common—is shame. We may teach and preach a theology of God's love, forgiveness, and grace, but we often resist accepting that forgiveness and grace for ourselves. Hypocrisy? Or a gap between our espoused theory and our practice? Often our espoused theology cannot overcome the theology by which we actually live, and the response to the exposure of our error is shame.

We were created as growing, learning creatures held precious in God's eyes. We are still in formation, becoming the people God wants us to be. Rather than understanding that our task is to grow (and *not* to be perfect), we experience the judgment of error as though we ourselves *were* errors. If that experience of shame is the painful consequence of being able to recognize the gap and experience the cognitive dissonance, it is understandable that people would avoid perceiving the gap—and thus avoid dealing with the shame.

Shame undercuts our very being as people. But there is an alternative response. Confronting the gap between our stated values and our practices can open a door of opportunity. We can experience the gap as a demand for change. Recognizing the need for change may not be as troubling as the response of shame, but it is discomforting nonetheless.

The Choice for Change

We are talking about bringing into awareness that which is already known to us, and clearly discerned by us in others. That awareness invites change. We are not talking about the deep psychodynamic changes pursued in psychotherapy. We are talking about choice. Some of the actions and beliefs we have learned do not serve us well. Without reflection we have incorporated practices that cause us sometimes to be incongruent, and sometimes to be ineffective, even in situations when we could have known and done differently. Our blindness has kept us from seeing our own wisdom and resourcefulness.

The rabbi already had the wisdom about the need to try something new if the old way wasn't working. He may even have acted on it in other circumstances. Had he acted on it in this case, he would have been able to make a difference.

Action science broadens our understanding of behavior to include our actions *and* the thinking process that informs those actions. What data we take in, how we process it, and what actions we take are all related in our individual behavioral systems. Since all behavior is designed, and since awareness is a part of our behavior, then unawareness, or blindness, is also designed. The presence of design suggests that other designs are possible and that we can become more aware. I believe that a key to dismantling this maladaptive behavior is to understand our thinking and reasoning processes.

We each respond the way we do to people and events because of the meaning we make of them and the impact those meanings make on us. We are very skillful. We think so quickly that our responses often seem instantaneous. But we can learn how to slow those processes down. If we can retrieve the reasoning, the assumptions, and the meanings we have made that led us to ineffective, maladaptive, or defensive routines, we will have the skills and tools we need to construct alternatives.

If we learn how to retrieve our internal processing, we will have the skills and tools we need to construct alternatives. We are already controlled by our reasoning processes, but they are often unavailable to us and not subject to our scrutiny. Bringing them to awareness is a way to take charge of ourselves, and the ways in which we live with one another.

Repentance: A Change of Mind

The Greek word for "repentance" is *metanoia*, meaning "a change of mind." This book offers some new ways to think about yourself and the ways in which you relate to the world. This "change of mind" provides an alternative to shame and a positive incentive for embracing the learning and growing process. The experience of cognitive dissonance can be exhilarating, because it identifies the newest opportunity to grow in faith and enhance effectiveness.

Responding to the discomfort produced by cognitive dissonance with exhilaration may be difficult to imagine. Learners, upon discovering their own incompetence, commonly respond with hostility, if not denial. Cognitive dissonance, the discovery of incompetence, or any other confrontation resulting in the necessity to learn something new and engage in personal change—each of these most often produces unpleasant feelings.

I worked with a bright, mature ministerial intern, Andrea, who would refer to a student as being in the "one-down" position. I was perplexed. Whenever I offered her what I thought was helpful and insightful (if not brilliant) feedback, she would respond by, in effect, hunkering down. Discussion revealed that we had very different understandings of what it meant to be a learner. We therefore attributed quite different meanings to the learning event.

For Andrea, to be a learner was to be judged inadequate, incompetent, in a "one-down" position relative to the one who taught. In my world, to be a learner is the highest aspiration. Learning means that I have successfully identified places where I can grow and have discovered a strategy to achieve that growth. When Andrea and I had one of these revelatory "learning" moments, each of us in fact was feeling envious of the other. She envied my being in the "one-up" position relative to her. I envied her chance to discover something new and to learn the skills that would improve her practice. I did not understand or even grasp her embarrassment or resentment. I was projecting what would have been my own response of exhilaration. She did not understand why I kept creating these events, believing my intention was to flaunt my power and position.

Andrea is not unusual. For over ten years my teaching colleagues and I have been taking clergy through a case in which they are asked to evaluate the performance of a particular minister. This minister has spoken to the church music director, whose performance has been judged inadequate by the board of deacons. Invariably the class evaluates the minister presented in the verbatim (word-for-word) case study as uncaring, unsympathetic, unpastoral, and ineffective. We write their evaluations on the chalkboard in front of the class. The evaluations remain on the board for the duration of the class.

We then ask the class to role-play an interaction between the minister and the deacons in which the minister comes in with the same verbatim and asks for feedback. The students playing the role of deacons inevitably re-produce the very behavior they have just judged as uncaring, unsympa-thetic, unpastoral, and ineffective. When we ask them why they would produce behavior which they know to be ineffective and which they have together just judged as ineffective, they are stumped.

Their designed blindness prevented them from seeing that they were reproducing behavior they knew would not work and which they had al-ready judged negatively in others. Confronted with their designed blindness and the companion behavior of designed incompetence, they responded variously. Over the years of repeating this exercise, I find that very few students have become excited and energized at the prospect of learning. Most students become upset and feel humiliated, set up, defensive, or an-gry. Some of them remained so for much of the year.

Most students, in time, undergo a profound change. What had at first felt humiliating appears as an opportunity. What had felt like hurtful con-frontation on the part of the instructors comes to be perceived as an act of support, caring, and deep respect. At the end of the course the most com-mon questions and concerns with which these students struggle are "How can I hold onto this new way of seeing and being and behaving in the world?" and "How can I retain this transformed state when I am working in a world in which good but broken people collude to keep each other blind?"

These are difficult questions. Amazing grace and increased skill may take people who once were blind and enable them to see and act differently in one particular scenario. The greater need is to recognize our persistent lack of reliably clear perception, and to learn how to peel back the blinders for ourselves. We need to move beyond the specifics of our own presenting case studies to a more generic model for understanding the world and our behavior within it. Then the learning we do is transportable and applicable to other situations in our lives. As long as we view each of our professional experiences of failure or error as idiosyncratic, one-time events, studying them will not yield us useful knowledge, and we will be caught repeating what we have not understood.

Developing generic models and identifying generic theories-in-use can sometimes appear to disregard the authentic uniqueness and individuality of the practitioner. That is a misunderstanding of the method. Each of these generic models is brought to life by people reflecting their own styles, and put forward in ways that reflect their own attitudes and experiences. The idiosyncratic ways in which people embody the models do not detract from our contention that most people's behavior is governed by rules, values, and meanings that can be mapped and known. In fact, when honed to their most pristine and simple form, these maps are shared as part of the social and cultural matrix in which we live and move and have our being.

The Model I World

With Argyris and Schon, we have chosen "Model I" as the name to describe the world as it is. The Model I world is constructed with values, goals, and strategies for realizing them. It is governed by rules of behavior; it makes meanings of the world and the people who inhabit it. It is the world with which we are familiar and into which we are thoroughly acculturated. Like the fish that swims surrounded by and dependent on its watery environment, we often cannot see our world. Model I is fraught with problems, and because of these problems, of which we are often unaware, the model gets us into trouble. Unaware of what is actually happening, we cannot learn.

How universal and how hard it is to perceive the patterns and break through them—a truth that becomes strikingly apparent when we look back to our biblical heritage.

The Psalms are filled with songs of self-pity, remorse, and lamentation, and with reports of the psalmist's feeling trapped and stuck with no way to turn. Sometimes the psalmist accepts responsibility, and sometimes the psalmist holds God responsible. It is helpful to remember Sister Gellerd's case. When working with her colleagues, her theory-in-use was:

- When I think something is important, withhold it.

- When angry at not being heard because I haven't said what is important to me:
    Blame others for not hearing what I haven't said.
    Hold them responsible for my lack of participation.
    Give up, withdraw politely, and wonder what is wrong with them.

The singer of Psalm 39 says:

I said, "I will guard my ways
    That I may not sin with my tongue;
I will keep a muzzle on my mouth
    As long as the wicked are in my presence.
I was silent and still;
    I held my peace to no avail;
My distress grew worse,
    My heart became hot within me.
While I mused, the fire burned;
    Then I spoke with my tongue [Ps. 39:1-3].

Sister Gellerd has joined a long and illustrious company of those who function out of this ineffective theory-in-use, who suffer the inner turmoil and burning fury as a result, and who hold others responsible, as we can see in the continuation of the psalm.

And now Lord, what do I wait for?
    My hope is in you.
Deliver me from all my transgressions,
    Do not make me the scorn of the fool,
I am silent; I do not open my mouth,
    For it is you who have done it.
Remove your stroke from me;
I am worn down by blows of your hand [Ps. 39:7-10].

Notice how the Apostle Paul tried to deal with the intuitive grasp he had of the dilemma caused by the gap between our professed beliefs and our behavior. In his letter to the Romans he observed:

I do not understand my own actions. For I do not do what I want, but I do the very thing I hate. Now if I do what I do not want, I agree that the law is good. But in fact it is no longer I that do it, but sin that dwells within me. ... For I do not do the good I want, but the evil I do not want is what I do. Now if I do what I do not want, it is no longer I that do it, but sin that dwells within me. So I find it to be a law that when I want to do what is good, evil lies close at hand [Rom. 7:15-17, 19-21].

Paul has progressed from blaming others, God, or other people, but he cannot quite claim the error fully without flinching. That is understandable. He is baffled by the awareness of two different theories or principles driving his actions and by his seeming inability to bring his theory-in-use (which manifests error) into line with his treasured and "wanted" espoused theory of good. So knowing that evil is present in the one who wants to do good, frustrated and embarrassed by the truth, he bravely acknowledges it, but at a distance—not me, but sin within me. This acknowledgment, made publicly to his faith community, is a profound and helpful beginning. It illustrates both how difficult it is to break through the barriers of designed blindness and how, with faith and determination and a community to help, progress is possible.

The Model I world in which the psalmist and Paul lived is essentially the same as the world in which we live. It creates structures, expectations, and rules of behavior that produce error, and self-sealing loops of interactions from which escape is difficult. Interrupting the familiar but flawed patterns remains unlikely. We have already mentioned one of the most distinctive phenomena that help produce this dilemma—designed blindness. In the following chapters we will look at some of these other features of Model I behavior and flesh out the map of a Model I world. Through this book we hope that the reader will come to understand how this model of the world sets us up for error. It doesn't need to be so. We will offer an alternative.

CHAPTER 2

Trapped By Virtue

Sister Gellerd, as you will recall from chapter 1, presented a case about a meeting in which she felt frustrated, powerless, and disrespected. Upon reflection, she realized that a theory-in-use could be inferred from her behavior. It had governed her actions, although she was unaware she held that theory.

Trying to Be Good

We talked about designed blindness as the phenomenon that allowed her to engage in behavior that was neither effective nor logical, without experiencing the cognitive dissonance she would have felt had she been aware. Because she valued highly both logic and effectiveness, exposure of her theory-in-use was a source of great discomfort and embarrassment. It was also her window of opportunity to learn more about herself and the ways in which she designed her own incompetence.

To refresh your memory, Sister Gellerd's theory-in-use was:

- When I think something is important, withhold it.

- When angry at not being heard because I haven't said what is important to me:
  Blame others for not hearing what I haven't said.
  Hold them responsible for my lack of participation.
  Give up, withdraw politely, and wonder what is wrong with them.

What would have led Gellerd to engage in such a preposterous strategy, even unaware? What must she have believed for such a choice to have seemed attractive, even on an unconscious level?

Social Virtues and Model I

One of the central factors explaining this and other disconcerting behaviors in which she, and we, engage with others, is the way we understand social virtues. "Social virtues" is a term we have given[1] to a particular set of values and the practices produced by adherence to those values. There are obviously many virtues to which people subscribe, each with its own meanings and consequences for behavior. Some of these virtues are more compelling than others, and some more prevalent than others. We have chosen to focus on four that have appeared over time to be the most universal, and that therefore have the most impact on our common lives. They are, much like the air we breathe, assumed and hardly noticeable. Yet they bear examination and analysis, for within them resides the key to many of our frustrating and disconcerting experiences of professional ineffectiveness.

Four social virtues are pivotal in constructing our interactions with others:

1. Be helpfully supportive.
2. Respect people.
3. Be strong.
4. Maintain integrity.

As virtues embodied in our individual behavior and embraced in our worldview, they are personal. Yet because embracing these virtues results in particular interactive behaviors, affecting interpersonal relationships and the organizations and environments in which these relationships occur, they all are ultimately social in practice. These social virtues are valued in every human culture in which action science has been used.[2] Extensive global travel, research, and work with foreign exchange students have found these social virtues to be consistently understood in the same way, resulting in a common human practice. They also, as we shall see, result in a common human dilemma. We have called this behavioral world as we know it Model I.

To understand Gellerd's behavior as a good and virtuous woman, it is important to understand the social virtues that drive and inform her and us as we do what we do: strive to be effective, good, and faithful practitioners.

MODEL I SOCIAL VIRTUES

1. Helpfully support people.
   This means:
   - Offer approval and praise.
   - Tell them what they want to hear.
   - Minimize disapproval and blame.

2. Respect people.
   This means:
   - Do not challenge others people's reasoning processes.
   - People's reasoning processes are undiscussable.

3. Be strong.
   This means:
   - Show capacity to hold your position in the face of another's advocacy.

4. Maintain integrity.
   This means:
   - Stick to your values and principles.
   - Don't cave in.

The Dilemma

The first social virtue is: helpfully support people, which means:

- Offer approval and praise.
- Tell them what they want to hear.
- Minimize disapproval and blame.

It was this social virtue that led Gellerd to withhold opinions that she thought were important. Even as she was judging the other participants in the meeting to be wrong, she also felt it was important—as their colleague and friend and as a religious person under vows—that she be supportive of them. Since she could not offer approval (because she disapproved), and since she wished to minimize disapproval and blame, she simply said nothing. She told them some of the facts of the case, which she felt they were willing to hear. She withheld her feelings or commitments, which they appeared not to want to hear.

So Gellerd was embodying the virtue of help and support by withholding what she thought was important. In the mode of common cultural wisdom and practice, she followed the maxim, "If you don't have something nice to say, don't say anything at all." Unfortunately, this maxim is a design for frustration and deceit. The Model I understanding of the social virtue that undergirds and sustains it, "Be helpfully supportive," often leads to disaster. Vital information is withheld because it is perceived as "not having something nice to say."

The second social virtue is to respect people, which means:

- Do not challenge other people's reasoning processes.
- People's reasoning processes are undiscussable.

It was important to Gellerd to respect the people gathered at the meeting, including one who was her superior. Therefore, when she heard them making assessments and determinations that she believed to be in error, she did not speak up and challenge their reasoning processes. She respected the taboo. Because people's reasoning processes are undiscussable, she was prevented from asking them to reveal theirs. As a respectful and virtuous person, she felt constrained from revealing her own. Withholding what was important to her stemmed from her belief that people who respect one another do not question, challenge, or discuss their reasoning processes. Gellerd's fuller knowledge of the family in question and a personal experience that had allowed her to develop a deeper sympathy and understanding were undiscussable. Bringing up these topics would have been deemed inappropriate, unprofessional, and disrespectful of the people and their roles in that setting. As a respectful professional, Gellerd was compelled to refrain from asking or telling about reasoning processes.

The third social virtue is to be strong, which means:

- Show capacity to hold your position in the face of another's advocacy.

It was here that Gellerd became caught in a quandary. She tried to advocate for her pupil but was prevented from doing so effectively by the constraints of the other social virtues. Unable to discover a way she could advocate successfully without sharing her reasoning or asking for theirs, she simply continued to repeat what was deemed appropriate, despite its futility. Consequently, she felt like a failure. Instead of being a credible and effective advocate for the child, she felt dismissed, discounted, and as helpless as the child himself.

This common understanding of strength is particularly destructive and problematic because it is inherently anti-learning. If being strong means that you hold to your position in the face of others' advocacy, regardless of the data or wisdom they may bring to the table, then being strong means that you are incapable of being influenced, and in some ways you are uneducable. Small wonder that strength and stupidity are often depicted in humor as going hand-in-hand.

The fourth social virtue is to maintain integrity, which means:

- Stick to your values and principles.
- Don't cave in.

This understanding of integrity is the other half of the preceding virtue, being an ally of "strength." It too is anti-learning for essentially the same reasons. If listening, learning, and incorporating new ideas are perceived as "caving in" or being unable to live up to one's principles, then to maintain integrity, one must shut out any credible information that might cause a change of mind. A folk-humor take on the behavioral consequences of such a value is the saying "My mind is made up. Don't confuse me with the facts."

We have often heard it said that leaders who were persuaded to change their minds demonstrated a lack of integrity—not that they demonstrated an ability to learn. We shackle our leaders and hobble creative problem-solving processes in public as well as private discourse when we understand integrity and strength as advocacy that is impermeable to influence.

Once again, as with the virtue of strength, Gellerd was unable to live up to the demands of the virtue of integrity. She felt troubled and inadequate. She was seemingly unable to stick to her principles. In the end she was outmaneuvered and outvoted; she caved in. The group was able to maintain an illusion of agreement because Gellerd valued helping and supporting her colleagues. This trait prevented her from telling them what they did not want to hear and from sharing with them her disapproval and the blame she attributed to them for what could be the waste of a child's mind and life.

Gellerd could have chosen to exhibit integrity and strength. She could have been a more forceful advocate for the child. She could have stated her values, the principles upon which she was building her position, and the reasoning that led her to believe that her proposal was the right thing to do. She could have asked the others to sign on to her understanding of what living up to proper educational principles would encompass, or to share their reasons for not doing so. She could have done all of that and felt virtuous as a person acting with strength and integrity. She would also have felt mean, uncaring, unsupportive, and disrespectful of her friends and colleagues, about whom she did care and with whom she had to work. Had she chosen the route of integrity and strength, her position might have prevailed, and she might have won the desired services for the child, but she would have felt like a failure nonetheless. To Gellerd the victory would have been empty because the cost was too high. The relationships that would have borne the cost were important to her.

Set Up for Failure

So we begin to see what has set Gellerd up and continues to set us up: We have been taught by our parents and our society to be people of virtue. We have also been taught what those virtues are to mean as they are played out in our lives. The ways in which the virtues are to be embodied and put in practice, however, turn out to be mutually exclusive. We can choose to be helpful, supportive, and respectful. *Or* we can be strong people of integrity. But we cannot be all four at the same time.

Consequently, no matter how hard to we try to be good, we always have to make choices that embrace behavior we would judge as bad. The conflict we experience in trying to be good and virtuous is designed into the social virtues. It is no wonder that we feel like failures even when we are trying hard to be good. The options we have been taught do not serve us in stressful situations. The limits contained within our map of the world contain us too.

Before Columbus sailed across the Atlantic and Magellan demonstrated that the earth could be circumnavigated, Europeans restricted their movements, explorations, and discoveries to the world they could see, the one that lay within the horizon. They could not conceive of any other options. As with the old-world Europeans, we are restricted by the model of the world we have learned. The world with which we are concerned here is the one of human interactions. Rather than allowing us to gather the maximum information, our model compels us to make untenable choices. We cannot fulfill the demands the social virtues place on us. It is not possible to be helpfully supportive and respectful while simultaneously exhibiting integrity and strength. We must always choose to be both good and bad at the same time. There is no other option on this map; the model has set us up, every one of us. To protect ourselves from the feelings of outrage, frustration, and judgment, we develop skills in designing blindness, protecting ourselves from a world that wounds and offers no balm for healing.

Dyer also was caught in the wish to embrace mutually exclusive social virtues. To be helpfully supportive of the staff, in a Model I way, she would have had to tell the staff what they wanted to hear and minimize her negative feelings and blame. She could have simply told them that in her meeting with the personnel committee, she had been told that the staff wanted the committee to use the merit-raise system. She could have ignored the fact that she had been sent with a different message, pretending that the original discussion had never happened. She might even have used the staff meeting to confirm with them that the personnel committee had understood them correctly. And she would have been understood as helpfully supportive, respectful, and probably "ministerial."

Dyer would have felt otherwise, however. She would have felt foolish and weak, her integrity compromised. Had she not said anything, had she let the discrepancy go, Dyer would not have felt "ministerial," because ministers act with integrity and moral strength. To allow what she saw as consensus and an implicit covenant to be broken or dismissed without acknowledgment or discussion would compromise basic principles of her faith—

principles she believed to be the cornerstone of faithful congregational life.

So Dyer made the choice that Gellerd did not—to go for the strength and integrity virtues first. She did present her reasoning and questioned the reasoning of the others. They reacted as people who had been treated with disrespect; they felt unsupported by the one who was supposed to be their advocate. She violated the rules of appropriate professional behavior by expressing disapproval and discussing the undiscussable.

The staff members responded by shutting down. They held fast to the virtues of helpful support and respect, and grew angry with Dyer for her violation. She felt caught, and responded with increased advocacy, thereby generating increased resistance on their part. The staff members protected each other by behaving respectfully—experienced by Dyer as concealing. She attributed to them the maintenance of a hidden agenda. The more she operated out of strength and integrity, the more they judged her by the values of support and respect, furthering their distance, increasing their distrust, and generating untested attributions about one another's feelings and intent. They were all in a double bind but unable to perceive it, unable to get out, and perpetuating a cycle of escalating error.

Levy also found himself constrained by the embedded conflict in the social virtues, as did the women of the sisterhood. Levy was strong. He continued to advocate for his position—his diagnosis and solution for their problem, despite their resistance. And he was a man of integrity. He was tenacious. He stuck to his values, his perceptions, his solutions, his principles. He did not give in. He was a virtuous man. Meanwhile, the virtuous women of the sisterhood were respectful. They did not challenge their rabbi's reasoning. Even though he was obviously working from a fatally flawed perception that rendered his solutions unacceptable, the women were silent. Rather than question his reasoning and illustrate for him the places where he had erred, they respectfully watched him continue to spin his wheels and generate unhelpful suggestions.

The women grew bitter and resentful as he persisted in behavior that was so clearly useless and unsupportive. He was neither telling them what they wanted to hear nor offering them approval and praise. In fact, by the solutions he advocated, they perceived (correctly) that he was intimating disapproval and suggesting that they were to blame for their problem. From their position, he appeared to be "blaming the victim"—that is, holding these good, well-intentioned women responsible for bad things that were happening to them. Rather than hearing sympathy in his fountain of suggestions, they felt negative judgment. The more he tried to "fix it," the worse they felt, because fixing it was not what they had come to him for.[3]

Is it any wonder that they found him incredibly mean and uncaring? He was withholding the help and support for which they asked. And as people who had chosen to embrace as their guiding virtues help, support, and respect, they found themselves constrained from communicating to the rabbi what he was doing that was so devastating. After all, if congregants learn nothing else about propriety, they learn that it is important to treat the rabbi with respect. And thus, one more time good people are set up for disaster and escalating error from which they cannot escape.

Why the Social Virtues Are So Hard to Change

As has become obvious, the social virtues we took in with our mother's milk and assimilated in much the same unconscious fashion did not prove to be as useful and nutritious as we had believed. We have great difficulty discerning the contradictions and double binds that govern our behavior. All of us operate in the same environment with our behaviors grounded in the same problematic premises. We think we are practical, reasonable, and in touch with reality. We cannot tell that we are governed by constructs we have learned and will pass on. A story relevant to this point was told by the Hasidic Rabbi Nachman of Breslov nearly 200 years ago.[4]

> One day the prime minister came into the presence of the King and announced that the grain supply of the kingdom was mysteriously poisoned. All who ate of the crop would go mad. The King ordered that the grain be destroyed. "But, your majesty," said the minister, "then all in your kingdom will starve."
>
> "Then let the people eat of the grain," said the King. "All save you and me. We will retain our sanity." "But your Majesty," replied the minister. "If all go mad save you and me then the people will think us mad and surely put us to death."
>
> "Then we too will eat of the grain," said the King, "but we will mark our foreheads with a sign so that when we see each other we will remember that we are mad."

It would seem that we have all eaten of the grains that produce madness (or at least designed blindness and predictable incompetence), but we

have forgotten to put marks on our foreheads to remind us that we participate in madness. I suggest to you that rather than mark ourselves and
accept the destiny of these madness-producing social virtues, we reconstruct them in ways that will enhance our effectiveness, enable us to detect
error, and produce healthier, more sustainable outcomes.

A warning is needed, however: The rest of the world will remain
"mad." I am inviting you into the dilemma faced by the prime minister and
the king. And you, with them, will have the choice—to choose madness
and assimilation or clarity, effectiveness, and the ability to see the world
and its people differently from the others with whom you live and love and
work. I hope that in time some of those with whom you work will be interested in this other way of seeing, thinking, and doing, and will learn with you
to discern the mark of wisdom from the mark of madness.

Knowing that I am inviting you into a new and therefore somewhat
disorienting world, I offer you Model II and its alternative social virtues. It
will challenge your assumptions and, if put into practice, will change your
behavior, your outcomes, and your relationships.

Model II Social Virtues

The alternative (Model II) social virtues have the same names as those in
Model I but carry different meanings, lead to different conclusions, and
therefore are embodied in different ways. The results can be startling. You
may even recognize that on some occasions you have done them all before.

MODEL II SOCIAL VIRTUES

1. Helpfully support people.
    This means:
    - Help individuals to become aware of the reasoning processes.
    - Help them become aware of gaps and inconsistencies.

2. Respect people.
    This means:
    - Human beings are capable of and interested in learning.

3. Be strong.
    This means:
    - Behavior reflects a high capacity for advocacy coupled with a high capacity for inquiry and vulnerability without feeling threatened.

4. Maintain integrity.
    This means:
    - Advocate and act on your point of view in such a way as to encourage confrontation and inquiry into it.

In a Model II world, helpfully supporting people means:

- Help individuals to become aware of their reasoning processes.
- Help them become aware of gaps and inconsistencies.

In such a model, the rabbi's intention to help and support the women in the sisterhood would produce very different actions. Had he been working from Model II virtues, he would have inquired as to what they wanted. He would not have assumed that he knew what help would mean for them, and would instead have asked them to tell him what specific help they were seeking. If their requested help appeared to him inconsistent with their stated goal, he would have identified that perceived gap, and asked about it. *Note*: He would have *asked* about it, because what appeared to him as a gap or inconsistency might have been a cue that he hadn't fully understood them and needed to inquire further to be sure. In the process of inquiry, he would have become clear about what they wanted, and they would have been helped to recognize any gaps or inconsistencies. Then the sisterhood would have been able to decide how it wished to reconcile those gaps, and the rabbi would have been able to decide if he could help them. In such a scenario the decision of what form help should take, and the choice of priorities that such decisions might require, reverts to the women, helping them to become more effective.

Respecting people in a Model II way means:

- Human beings are capable of and interested in learning.

This model of respect works very nicely with help and support. If Levy had provided the kind of help and support to the sisterhood just described, and they had been given the tools and the responsibility for clarifying and defining their own understanding of help, they would have learned something about themselves and their organization, possibly brought their desires and expectations more into alignment, and maintained responsibility for the agenda and success of their organization. In short, beginning with the assumption that they could learn and that they were interested in doing so would have resulted in their being treated as fully competent adults, respected managers, and problem-solvers, co-creators with the rabbi.

Being strong in Model II means:

- Behavior reflects a high capacity for advocacy coupled with a high capacity for inquiry and vulnerability without feeling threatened.

This virtue is difficult to grasp. We tend either to advocate or to inquire. It is difficult to balance our behavior so that we are both advocating our position—a necessity if we are to be clear and to avoid hidden agendas—and inquiring authentically and openly about the positions and understandings held by others. The art of being able to stand in a position with comfort and vulnerability—ready to share our reasoning and to promote our position while openly listening to others, actively learning, and being changed in the process—is a skill-based craft. In addition to changing the way in which we think about strength, we must practice.

Maintaining integrity in a Model II way is similarly difficult. It means:

- Advocate and act on your point of view in such a way as to encourage confrontation and inquiry into it.

This virtue is so countercultural that it presents a significant challenge. It requires that we think very differently about why we are holding and presenting an opinion. Integrity means that we hold opinions until such time as we discover they are in error. That discovery is of importance to us. It is not so much about being right as it is about the discovery of truth. Embracing Model II strength will produce countercultural behavior, which may confuse those around us. It is difficult to credibly invite inquiry into our own reasoning. It is not what people expect of us.

We can more easily conceive of Model II strength because we have witnessed or participated in it within the context of debates. Effective debating requires that we engage in effective inquiry, because our best defense is to understand the opposition. But when we engage Model II integrity, we are pushing the familiar into new territory. The exercise of integrity includes not only being able to put forth our own position and actively inquire about the other's position; it demands in addition that we actively encourage, even desire that others confront us and press their own inquiries to us. The reasons are multiple.

First, it is just. If we believe that it is useful to inquire of and confront others about their position and reasoning processes, then we must encourage others to behave the same way toward us. We want to be respected and want people to assume that we are capable of learning. We indeed are interested in learning—and how better to learn than to invite others to inquire and confront us about our positions and reasoning? We desire help and support from those with whom we work—meaning that we will want them to help us identify errors, gaps, and inconsistencies in our reasoning. If we truly believe that these behaviors are virtuous, then we will wish to enjoy the benefits of them ourselves. Finally, if we are concerned about effectiveness and committed to being learners, we must encourage people to tell us what they see and hear us doing. Ultimately, becoming wise and skillful learners is our lifeline to sustainable effective ministry. We will be indebted to the people who willingly hold up reflective mirrors, that we might see ourselves as others see us—errors, gaps, inconsistencies, and all.

Assured of God's love and God's grace, we can recognize these people as precious messengers of the Most High.

Positioned for Success

Thus it is possible to embrace and embody all the social virtues at the same time. With this reconstructed understanding, the social virtues take on an internal consistency. We are less likely to perceive the need to protect ourselves from the cognitive dissonance that originally led us to design blindness into our behavior. Beginning with these new meanings of the social virtues, we recognize that it is not rules that create rigidity but how the rules are understood. We realize that there is a way of moving, being, and interacting with the world that is both rule-bound and open to learning. The rules, rather than serving rigidly to maintain the world as we know it or believe it to be, serve to help us hold that world and its meanings up to careful scrutiny and reexamination. The rules of Model II social virtues presume a learning, seeking practitioner who is more interested in discovering the truth than in being right, more interested in being effective than in having control. That priority is very different from that to which we are accustomed.

Model II Virtues and Biblical Faith

Those values and the behaviors engendered by them are aligned with biblical faith, which would have us be humble learners and servants to that which is holy. That faith values justice over "rightness." That biblical faith recognizes and honors the freedom of the spirit to move in every person, and exhorts us not to control that which is not ours to control. As the prophet Micah said so plainly, faithfulness requires us "to do justice, love kindness and walk humbly with our God" (Micah 6:8). We are not required to be in control of others, only of ourselves. We are charged to be *effective* in our faithfulness, encouraged to be accountable for the effects of our behavior. As we hear in the gentle reminder of the Apostle Paul, "All things are lawful . . . but not all things are helpful" (1 Cor. 6:12, RSV).

These biblical verses are well known, but difficult to put into practice. Embracing these new understandings of the social virtues and the behaviors to which they lead requires the willingness, should the need arise, to open up to inquiry and testing all that we assume and all the truths we cherish. The task can be daunting, unnerving, intimidating, and exhilarating. The invitation to transformation always is.

We have considered the ways in which Model I social virtues were manifested in the scenarios we explored, and the ways in which they provided a design for frustration, ineffectiveness, and a lowering of self-esteem. That is because these social virtues operate in a predictable way that is repeated no matter what the context, to the extent that the Model I social virtues are at play. It can be mapped in this way:

Predictable Patterns of Model I

Social virtues inform our behavior. We can choose either model. Whichever model we choose will produce values consistent with that model that govern our behavior.

Model I social virtues produce *governing values* for action, which operate in this way:

- Achieve purposes as the *actor* perceives them.
- Maximize winning and minimize losing.
- Minimize eliciting negative feelings.
- Help one to be rational and minimize emotionality.

These governing values lead to the following action strategies:

- Design and manage the environment so that the *actor* is in control of factors relevant to him or her.
- Own and control the task.
- Unilaterally protect oneself.
- Unilaterally protect others from hurt.

These action strategies produce the following behavioral consequences:

- Actor seen as defensive.
- Defensive interpersonal and group relationships.
- Defensive norms.
- Low freedom of choice, internal commitment, and risk-taking.

All of which produces:

- Decreased effectiveness.[5]

The self-sealing loop goes on unbroken, and we are highly skilled at remaining unaware.

We can see how and why our skillful clergy practitioners got caught in a cycle which they could neither escape from nor improve upon. Using the Model I social virtues results in this antilearning set of governing principles, which in fact require remarkable skill to implement. Unfortunately, when what we are doing isn't working and something else is needed, we put our effort into doing more and more of what we have already done, and doing it even better. It becomes skilled incompetence, of which we are unaware.

Predictable Patterns of Model II

The Model II social virtues offer an alternative. When rigorously adhered to, they can lead to a process that has the capacity to be self-correcting, learning-enhanced and effective. When mapped, the predictable process looks like this:

Model II social virtues produce *governing values* for action which operate in this way:

- Seek valid and validatable information.
- Maximize free and informed choice.
- Invest internal commitment to the choice and constant monitoring of its implementation.

These in turn lead to the following action strategies:

- Design situations or environments where participants can be original and can experience high personal causation (psychological success, validation, experience of being essential).
- Control task jointly.
- Protect self through joint enterprise and with orientation toward growth (participants speak in directly observable data categories, seek to reduce own blindness about inconsistency and incongruity).
- Bilaterally protect others.

These action strategies produce the following behavioral consequences:

- Actor experienced as minimally defensive.
- Minimally defensive interpersonal relations and group dynamics.
- Learning-oriented norms: trust, individuality, open confrontation on difficult issues.

These behaviors produce the following consequences for learning:

- Testable processes that can be confirmed or disconfirmed.
- Double-loop learning.
- Public testing of theories.

With these consequences for the quality of life:

- Quality of life is more positive than negative.
- Effectiveness of problem solving will be great, especially for difficult problems.

All of which produces:

- Increased long-run effectiveness.[6]

Oh, theories are interesting, you may be thinking, but what would it *look* like to put them into practice? We return to Temple Torah. How might things have gone differently for Levy if he had operated out of Model II social virtues and designed a strategy in response to the sisterhood that was informed by those virtues?

To begin with, the rabbi would have *thought* differently. He would have constructed the situation in his mind differently. Rather than understanding himself as the wise "fixer" of their problem, he would have seen himself as a co-learner, a co-creator with them. And he would have begun with wondering what it was they wanted and how he might contribute. In other words, he would have begun his thinking process with inquiry, rather than with assumptions about the sisterhood, and he would have understood building an agenda as a task they shared jointly, to be made public and tested, rather than creating one himself and then trying to engineer them into accepting it. He would have begun with other beliefs as well. He would have believed that learning from this enterprise was possible for both himself and the sisterhood. They were all capable of learning, and were in fact interested in it. Beginning with that belief about himself, he would be positioned to be authentically curious and open.

Having those different beginning theories of action in his belief system, he would have been moved to act in distinctly different ways. He would have begun with inquiry in an effort to gather valid information that could be confirmed. He would have asked the women what kind of help they wanted, what form useful help would take, asking them for specificity and the kind of an outcome they sought. He could have continued his inquiry until the information gathered was specific enough that he had clear validatable data—an outcome that could be tested and evaluated. He could also ask why they believed that outcome would serve them, seeking to understand and make explicit their reasoning. He could then advocate for his own perception about what kind of intervention on his part might be helpful, and offer his reasoning. He would encourage them to challenge and raise questions about his position, as he had inquired about theirs. In a setting such as this, each party is advocating for his or her position in a way that is open to inquiry, and each is not only learning about the other's perception but is discovering gaps in his or her own reasoning process. A common shared understanding about the situation emerges.

Out of that common understanding develop a joint control of the agenda and the definition of the problem to be solved. With that collaboration come shared creativity and generation of ideas. With the shared ownership of possible strategies comes a joint exploration of the possible consequences and outcomes of a variety of solutions. A shared investment in and responsibility for the solution and its implementation develops, as well as a shared interest in evaluating the outcome and learning from and improving agreed-on strategies.

In this new scenario, a Model II interaction, the rabbi and the sisterhood are no longer adversaries. They are not locked into making negative evaluations based on private and untested attributions each has made about the other. Instead they are allies on the same team, attempting to achieve common goals by the exercise of mutual support, respect, integrity, and strength. Together they learn from and improve the strategies they have adopted.

A caveat. But it might not have worked out that way. The rabbi could have encountered resistance. Although the rabbi's behavior was governed by Model II social virtues, the women of the sisterhood might have continued to function with their own model intact. It is not only possible but likely, particularly if this is the first time Levy has responded to them in such a way. The possibility of learning, however, would remain, at the minimum on the part of the rabbi. Additionally, opportunities for learning would exist for the women of the sisterhood who chose to take them. The resistance offered by the women would also be different from what the rabbi had previously encountered, because it would be generated in response to a different situation.

Operating within the context of the Model II social virtues demands that there be no unilateral control of the agenda. The desire for control is replaced by a design to generate and share information, including information about what the various participants would like. The rabbi could begin by being open about his desire for this kind of sharing. He could continue his advocacy coupled with authentic inquiry, so that the solutions he advocated would change as his information and understanding increased. He could also encourage the women to ask questions. He might even state directly that he would find their questions helpful and supportive, because unless they helped him understand why he was not being helpful, he could not change.

The ability of the group, including the rabbi, to detect errors is enhanced the more open the rabbi is about (1) his reasoning, (2) his willingness to entertain questions, and (3) his interest in finding out exactly what the women want and are interested in. To the extent that the rabbi combines this behavior with openly gathering and sharing data, inviting them into the informed process of shaping the agenda and planning how to proceed, the likelihood of engaging in self-sealing ineffective behavior diminishes.

Not all of the interaction needs to be governed by Model II. Not all of the participants need to be aware of the ways in which their understanding of the social virtues sets them up for error. Any little change provides an increased opportunity for detecting error and learning. Every little inquiry adds to the information available and allows for public testing. With an increase in information and inquiry comes a commensurate decrease in the amount of inference and attribution on which people are basing their judgments. With every inquiry, clearer decisions are made, and errors are less likely to occur and more likely to be discovered. Model II doesn't need to be practiced perfectly to have a positive effect.

Another caveat. It is true that some of the women in the sisterhood may experience the rabbi's new behavior as rude. They may become defensive. The rabbi cannot control their responses. But if they become defensive, the question before Levy is: What should he do with their defensiveness? To the extent that he can avoid becoming defensive in return and instead can remain curious, interested, and open, he can continue to ask questions that help him understand. Responding to defensiveness by voicing curiosity, he enhances the credibility of his interest in understanding them and his genuine desire to be helpful. There are no guarantees.

But the rabbi will have avoided escalating defensiveness, maximizing his chances of being effective. A related consequence: He has created a trail of awareness by which he can reconstruct his reasoning, check and test his own behaviors and assumptions, and detect his own errors. By using the data produced by such open and free-flowing feedback loops, continuous corrections are possible and high levels of effectiveness can be maintained.

This chapter has presented challenges to your thinking as well as your behavior. It is a lot to absorb. To understand what this new world of Model II might hold for you and how the social virtues can transform your behavior and heighten your effectiveness, you must begin to try them. Start simply, in situations in which you feel relatively safe. Pay attention to feedback from others. Even when you have not solicited it, that feedback conveys important information to you about the effects of your behavior. This information is itself powerful learning.

CHAPTER 3

Knowing What You Know

Lewis Carroll, in his book *Alice's Adventures in Wonderland*, captures our frustrations with the struggle to communicate clearly, especially when confronted with a situation in which the assumptions and values are not shared, or are shifting. Alice's experience may feel somewhat like your own.

> "[Y]ou should say what you mean," the March Hare went on.
> "I do," Alice hastily replied; "at least I mean what I say—that's the same thing, you know."
> "Not the same thing a bit!" said the Hatter. "Why, you might just as well say that 'I see what I eat' is the same thing as 'I eat what I see'!"
> "You might just as well say," added the March Hare, that 'I like what I get' is the same thing as 'I get what I like'!"

By now you may be feeling disoriented, somewhat intrigued, and even a little defensive. That is natural. We are talking about one of the most important and precious parts of your life—your professional practice and your faithfulness to that call. We have invited you into a world that may seem almost imaginary, a fantasy, a world in which what you thought you knew to be true is questioned, and what you thought you knew to be effective is flawed—almost like taking the journey Alice took through the looking glass, a journey in which all perceptions needed to be tested. Or it may be like stepping into a house of mirrors in which what you think you see is not necessarily what is there.

These feelings are reasonable. I am asking you to become like Alice, who crossed the threshold through the looking glass into a world that looked like the one she knew but was deceptively different. Just as Alice had to check out every assumption she made about others and the meanings of their communications to function effectively, I suggest that you do the same. I wish you to test your perceptions and reconsider the obvious. And I ask you to step into a house of mirrors. Actually I am asking you to create your own house of mirrors into which you will then step. The mirrors are created as you solicit the perceptions of others, perceptions about you and about the consequences, intended and otherwise, of your behaviors.

When I was learning to drive, I had to learn how to steer the car, engage the clutch, shift the gears, modulate the speed, look out the windshield at what was ahead of me, look in the rearview mirror to see what was coming from behind, look in the side mirrors to know what was happening alongside of me, and pay attention to what, if anything, might be in a path of intersection or collision. It was mind-boggling and overwhelming. Just when I was understanding what I was seeing in the rearview mirror, I'd realize that I had not looked forward for quite some time. Or, thrilled with my ability to move smoothly into the next gear as I was pulling out, I would forget to check my side mirror for other vehicles that might be in my trajectory. Finally, I learned to put all these elements together well enough to pass my driver's test and receive a license. But it was many months before I felt that I could proceed at a reasonable speed while performing all of those functions simultaneously and with adequate skill.

As experienced practitioners, you know that the terrain in which you work speeds by, whether you are ready or not. Often you intuitively switch gears without being aware of the stimuli or the reasoning behind the decision. Your actions and responses are automatic. When you are humming along on familiar turf, it as though you were functioning on cruise control. You may hardly notice the decisions you make while driving. As a consequence, it is difficult to retrieve the errors when something goes wrong. I am offering you more mirrors than in an ordinary car. It will take time to learn how to use them. You have been whizzing along on this highway for a long time—but only with limited visibility and few corrective mirrors. In time you will remember to use the new devices, and your driving will provide more than transportation—it will become a way of moving and being in the world.

Skilled Incompetence?

I have suggested that much of what you have learned to do is ineffective, and you have learned the skills to produce that ineffective behavior repeatedly and predictably. You have been trained in skilled incompetence. That notion is a lot to absorb. It is even more difficult to sort out. Changing the ways in which you function is a formidable task—and scary. You have probably functioned pretty well in your profession. Yet here I am suggesting that you perform in ways that reflect skilled incompetence, built-in error, and that you are blind to these facts.

But, you may protest, signs of your competence are everywhere. You can see the many successes of your ministry and find no compelling reason to make such radical assessments as those I suggest. Despite the questions and challenges I have raised, you may not desire to make such major changes. That is understandable. Most of the time, the way we function is adequate. We get the job done. We are successful practitioners. Most of the time.

This book is for the other times, the times when something went wrong and we don't know why. It speaks to the times when we cannot figure out how we could have done it differently or better. It is for those unpleasant events in our professional history that seem to recur, resurfacing in new situations like a bad penny. It is for those past events that nag at us, about which we ruminate or continue to feel uncomfortable. These are the events where we have not been able to understand what went wrong. Because we have not satisfied our need for understanding, we remain uneasy, wishing for clarity and resolution.

What we deal with here is helping to interrupt patterns of behavior that we know are ineffective, yet which get triggered anyway while we feel ourselves slipping helplessly out of control. At those times, we need something different. If we keep doing what we have always done, we will keep getting what we have always gotten. But we don't know how to detect the error in what we were doing and thus are at a loss to know just what different thing we ought to explore.

In those situations, at those times, when our blindness has sealed us off from seeing the whole and we feel stuck, Model II offers a way out. It is a way to break the cycle. We learn how to elicit information, identify resources, and encourage the challenges that can help. These skills can help us be more effective in the immediate situation and enable us to use that learning in the future.

I am offering you some tools, some alternative ways of thinking and of framing what is happening so that you might be able to interrupt the self-sealing cycle and learn new skills. But in a book I can only offer you knowledge. For this knowledge to be transformed into skills, you will need to practice and enlist the help of others.

Organized for Learning

The social-virtues grid provides the large organizing framework and is in some ways analogous to the shelving in your supply closet. It provides the conceptual context and the categories into which the tools are placed. These tools are helpful whenever they are practiced but will be most useful and effective when applied in the context of the Model II social virtues. Within this supply-closet framework are shelves and hooks on which the tools can hang. As you acquire these tools, you will find the right hooks and shelves for you to keep them in easy access. Each of these tools will work in the service of the Model II social virtues, giving you practical, retrievable methods to implement their application.

What Happened?

The first tools I offer you are the companion concepts of directly observable data (DOD) and the ladder of inference.

Larry and Martin served on a committee together. They were trying to redesign something that wasn't working well. Martin had an idea. Larry, a large and muscular man, hunched over with his chin on his hand and his elbows on the table. He furrowed his brow and appeared to grimace. Martin did not know Larry well, but feeling intimidated, he dropped the idea he had advanced and withdrew a little. The meeting continued with a few more ideas presented and then adjourned. The group did not discuss Martin's idea. He went home uncomfortable. He had thought his idea was a pretty good one. He didn't know why Larry thought it was so awful. But he liked Larry and didn't want to risk crossing him, knowing they had so many things on which they would be working together.

Eventually one of the other ideas that had been presented was adopted and put into operation.

A few months later Larry was sitting with Martin over coffee. "Martin," Larry said, "there is something I've been meaning to ask you. You had that great idea last spring when we were working on the new design, and almost as soon as you presented it, you withdrew it. I was really disappointed that you did that. I thought it was the best idea that had come forward."

Martin was stunned. "I stopped advocating for it when I could tell that it was making you angry. I didn't know what about it made you angry. I didn't take it off the table. I just wasn't invested enough in it to push. It was one idea among many and certainly not worth making you angry."

Larry now was the one who was stunned. "I never was angry. I don't know what you are talking about. And I thought for sure you had withdrawn the idea from discussion."

Martin and Larry each made observations about the other, and working from what they understood to be culturally normal, made inferences and attributions that were untested and proved to be untrue.

The directly observable data Martin thought he had was that Larry was angry. But Larry wasn't angry.

On retracing the scene, Martin recalled seeing Larry leaning on his palm, elbow on the table, forehead furrowed and face contracted. That meant angry in Martin's world but not in Larry's. That is how Larry looked when he was concentrating.

If Martin had checked out his inference, had said, "Larry, to me you look angry. Are you? Did something I say bother you?" Larry could have said, "No, I'm not angry, I'm thinking. Your idea intrigues me, and its implementation would suggest some other changes which might be fascinating. So I was concentrating, trying to follow the chain of events to their logical conclusion. Actually, I really like it."

On the other side, Larry, who really liked Martin's idea, had assumed that Martin had withdrawn it and no longer wished it to be discussed. Being respectful in a Model I way, Larry had not asked about that either.

Had he checked, the scene might have gone something like this: At the end of the meeting, as the chair of the committee summarized the options for people to think about, Martin's idea was not included. Larry could have said, "Excuse me, but Martin put out an idea which I found intriguing and which opened up whole new possibilities. Is there any reason why we cannot consider that as well? Martin, would you have any objections?"

With either of these two scenarios, a good idea would not have been jettisoned because of errors in interpretation of the directly observable data.

Directly observable data are what can actually be seen, heard, or captured concretely, such as the actual words spoken, gestures expressed, rapidity of speech, voice tone, volume, and body posture. These data do not include their meanings. Some meanings are culturally imposed. They are one rung up the ladder of inference. Other meanings are inferences based on what are understood to be culturally accepted meanings (such as how an angry face looks). Meanings always hold the possibility of error and can always be tested for validity. To detect error, you need to slow down your thinking (which is probably racing up the ladder of inference) to retrieve the actual directly observable data.

For example, in the scenario we have just described:

Directly observable data (DOD):

Furrowed forehead, contracted face, chin propped on arm and leaning heavily.

- *Inferred meaning:*
    Anger

- *Actual meaning:*
    Concentration

Directly observable data (DOD):

Martin stops advocating for his idea.

- *Inferred meaning:*
    Martin has withdrawn it.
    Martin does not want it discussed.

- *Actual meaning:*
    Martin thinks it has angered someone.
    Martin values the relationship more than the idea.

Sister Gellerd's Ladder of Inference

Sister Gellerd stopped advocating for her position in the meeting because people were interrupting and talking over her. As she reported in her case presentation, she could tell that they really didn't want to hear what she had to say anyway. They didn't value her opinion and probably did not think much of her expertise. She did not want to reinforce their poor opinion of her, so she pretended to acquiesce and withdrew.

This description of events was what Gellerd presented in her case as data. What it actually conveyed was data about Gellerd's ladder of inference, the meaning she made in her cultural context of the behaviors around her.

Gellerd could have checked out her inferences and attributions. She could have said, "I feel frustrated. Everyone is talking at once. Why are you speaking when I'm speaking?" One of the committee might have said, "I'm sorry. I didn't mean to offend you. I was just very engaged, and so as I began to see where you were going, I guess I jumped in."

The committee chair might have said, "This is such a sticky wicket, and we have so little time to deal with it. I thought the high level of energy was good, meant that everyone cared and was really invested. It seemed that allowing the talk and ideas to have the freedom of spontaneity was a way in which to do important work quickly, by not interrupting the flow. I'm sorry if it was preventing you from getting your thoughts out. Go ahead, finish what you were saying."

A very different outcome might have been achieved for the youngster involved as well as for Gellerd, and a team with at least a respectful understanding of one another's concerns, if not a common goal, might have been forged.

We can identify what happened in the race up the ladder of inference:

Directly observable data (DOD):

> People are speaking at the same time.
> When Sister Gellerd speaks, others are speaking also.

Inferred meaning:

> People don't respect each other.
> People don't respect Sister Gellerd.
> People don't value her opinion.
> People don't want to hear what she has to say.

Actual meaning:

> People are very engaged.
> People are in a hurry.
> People think they can listen and talk at the same time.
> People think she had already said what was important.
> Her membership on the team is valued.

When Gellerd traced her intervention back to the directly observable data, rather than to the meanings she had imposed, a whole range of possibilities opened up, and her freedom to move and make choices was greatly enhanced. No longer was she surrounded by people who undervalued her, her opinion, and her ministry; no longer was she forced to work with people who were rude, unsympathetic, and uncaring.

She discovered that she worked with people whose culture of engagement included talking when others were talking, and speaking over one another. This culture was new to her but certainly less hostile than she had thought, and capable of supporting sound ministry and great love.

Toby Dyer: A Lack of Data

Dyer's first mistake occurred prior to the staff meeting that "went wrong." She had a mistaken perception that consensus did exist. All of her behaviors, strategies, and responses were predicated on her assumption of an existing consensus—but that consensus was an imaginary one. Dyer had assumed consensus as a result of the meanings she made of the directly observable data—meanings that she never tested.

At the first staff meeting in which the alternative possibilities for distribution of salary increases were discussed, there were extended periods of silence. Dyer was not used to that. This was a staff that generally spoke quickly and easily without great silences. After the obvious options for distribution of salary increases had been laid out and brief comments were made by staff, the room grew silent.

When what seemed a reasonable amount of time had passed, Dyer concluded the meeting by stating that it appeared that the staff preferred an across-the-board design for the increase. She said that her conclusion was based on her having heard so many concerns expressed about the negative impact of merit raises on working relationships if the raises were perceived as putting staff in competition with each other. No one responded.

Dyer took the silence as confirmation that she had correctly summarized the staff position and announced that she would dutifully deliver the message to the personnel committee and advocate for the position.

If Dyer had simply stated her observation, that no one was talking any longer, and asked what that silence meant, she may have gotten responses like this:

We are not used to having this kind of discussion in a serious manner. We are used to spending some of our time together complaining. Sometimes we enjoy complaining together. It is bonding. This conversation about salaries feels difficult.

We are being asked to discuss something together which feels personally threatening. If I say what I think and feel and protect my own self-interest, my co-workers might be hurt or angry. I might sound selfish.

This is too big of a question to spring on us. I need time to think.

They never asked our opinion before. Why now? Do they want us to do their dirty work and make the hard decisions?

The truth is that Dyer had no idea what the people were thinking or feeling. They weren't telling, and she, out of her own need to have an answer for the personnel committee, invented a decision, blind to the fact that she was doing so.

We can identify what happened in the race up the ladder of inference:

Directly observable data:

Long silence after brief discussion.

• *Inferred meaning:*

They have decided.
The position with the fewest expressed objections is the preferred.
We have a consensus.

• *Actual meaning:*

They are in a quandary.
They don't know how to discuss this subject.
They don't feel comfortable discussing it.
They need time to think about it.
No option presented sounds good.

Dyer's anger and frustration, her feelings of betrayal and embarrassment, were based on the assumption that her data were correct, that the staff had come to a consensus. But we can now see that she was operating not on data but on a rung of the ladder of inference. No wonder staff members were confused and irritated by her righteous indignation. They didn't know what consensus she was talking about. They had never bought in.

The Rabbi's Misconception

Levy had moved to higher levels on the ladder of inference. His inference was reinforced and complicated by differences of gender culture as well as personal style. When the women of the sisterhood asked for help, Levy ran up the ladder of inference and assumed that they were asking him to fix their situation. His behavior was constructed around his belief that they had actually asked him to fix it—a misconception that accounts partly for the hard time he had discerning his error.

In the rabbi's mind, telling him the problem was identical to asking him to fix it. Not so for the women. For the women, telling him the problem was a way of connecting, of letting him know what was happening, of sharing and providing an opportunity for support and sympathy. The only datum was that they had told him their situation as they understood it. He believed, though, that he had received more.

We can identify what happened in the race up the ladder of inference:

Directly observable data:

Women report dissatisfaction about the sisterhood.

• *Inferred meaning:*

The members of the sisterhood are dissatisfied with their organization.
They want the rabbi to fix it.

• *Actual meaning:*

They are adjusting to change.
They want the rabbi to listen and to sympathize.

The Ladder of Inference

Look at the model of the ladder of inference shown below. The closest rung to the ground is the directly observable data (DOD). The farthest away is what those of us who weren't even there think about it (hearsay, third-party reports, opinions and discussion by those not present). Most of the time when we are acting, we do so from the third and fourth rungs, quite distant from the actual data that spurred the activity.

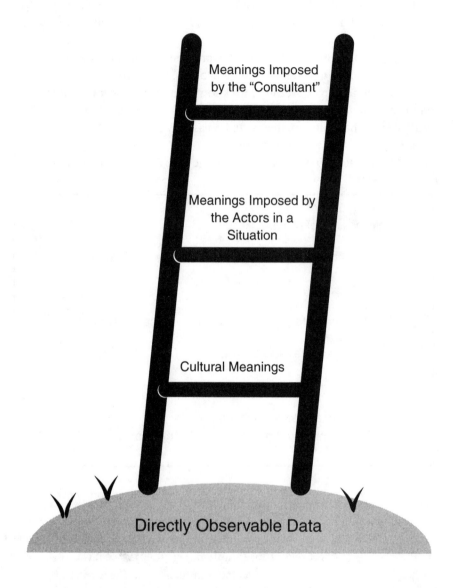

By the time one reaches the highest level of the ladder of inference, one is so far from the data that generated it that errors are unavoidable, unless the actor travels continuously up and down the ladder, confirming or disconfirming each new inference and attribution.

The "air" (data) up there at the top is thin. The only antidote to being "oxygen-deprived" (data-free) is to constantly review, recheck, and reconfirm what we believe to be true in a given situation against the directly observable data. Each time we do that checking, we can adjust, correct, or refine our understanding. Our decisions and our actions will be more responsive to the actual situation, and our effectiveness will increase.

When we know how to travel up and down the ladder of inference regularly, not only will the margin of error decrease; but when an error does occur, we will have learned the route by which to identify and correct it.

Learning Through Cues

Another tool that is helpful when trying to learn this new behavior is the technique of identifying "cues." We experience certain cues, either thoughts, words that come to mind, or feelings that trigger an automatic set of responses that often are self-sealed and unhelpful. Identifying those cues allows us to make a choice to let the familiar routine play itself out or to decide, "No, I'm not going there this time."

"Obviously": Signal of Untested Inference

For instance, one noticeable cue that we are scooting up the ladder of inference is that we are talking or thinking about something that happened and use the word, aloud or silently, "obviously." We probably wouldn't use the word "obviously" if it truly were obvious. Most often the word is a cover for an untested inference or attribution. "Larry was obviously angry." It may have been obvious to Martin, but it wasn't true.

Sometimes the primary actors share a common understanding, but those who are observing do not. Particularly if the situation is uncomfortable, these observers may find safety and comfort in the distance provided by climbing the ladder of inference.

For instance, in congregations with committees that rotate membership, often the newest people on the committee witness exchanges for which they have no history or context. Rather than breaking into the conversations and deliberations with questions, many will choose to sit back and watch. From that location they make inferences and attributions, and craft meanings that remain untested—meanings that become a force to be reckoned with, a "truth" in their experience.

These "truths" often generate and provide the focus for the unofficial parking-lot and kitchen conversations that drive so many churches. Such an event happened at First Church.

At First Church the minister, the Rev. Andrew James, and Leon Hopps, a congregant, have a long, close relationship. They love to wrestle with ideas. One night at a committee meeting they got into a debate that really heated up. They raised their voices, and everyone in the room got quieter.

It was really quiet when the committee members put away their coffee cups, nodded to the minister, and went home. Leon stayed a little after everyone else left and flung his arm around the minister's shoulders. "By God, that was fun!" he said. The two of them grinned and went home feeling good.

Two years later Claire Harris declined an offer to chair that committee. The reason given: "It is too scary and difficult to keep the meetings in order and restrain Reverend James from fighting with parishioners." Nobody could understand that response until someone sat down with this potential lay leader and listened to her story. She had attended the meeting at which James had obviously been ruthless in a disagreement with a parishioner without regard for his role as pastor. "It was terrifying," she said. "I could never stand that if it happened to me." Yet what was "obvious" to James and Hobbs, who had been involved in the argument, was that such an event would never have happened to Claire Harris. It had been an engagement by consent between two people who had a history and a relationship which they held in high and positive regard.

What was an "obviously" ruthless act to one was an "obvious" act of trust and intimacy to the other. Based on the meanings they imposed, Claire Harris had an authentic experience of watching a brutal verbal attack, while Leon Hobbs had an equally authentic experience of being trusted and special. Both experiences were conflicting versions of the same event.

The impact of living high up on the ladder of inference is not always of such weighty significance. In simple, everyday interactions, however, it affects us and can routinely shape our daily experience and compromise our decision-making.

Jen is another person surprised and caught unaware by her position high up the ladder of inference. The mother of small children, Jen recently took on a part-time job teaching aerobics at a gym near her home. One student, Sally, kept looking at the clock during her aerobics class. It was obvious to Jen, the new instructor, that Sally was hating the class and anxious for it to be over.

Jen worked harder and harder to make the class exciting, feeling more and more downcast as the hour went by. Sally kept looking at the clock every chance she got. At the end of class, as Sally ran out the door, she yelled out to Jen, "Thanks! That was great! I left something in the oven, but I was having such a good time, I decided to wait until the end of class to run home and turn it off. Hope it's not burnt!" So much for what is obvious.

Other Cues to Watch For

Sometimes the cue is a feeling, such as being embarrassed or humiliated. That is a good signal to help us recognize that we are probably experiencing this incident as though we were children. Often, such feelings are in response to an erroneous thought. When something happens and we think the meaning of the person's actions is obvious, it is easy to slide into a feeling response. When that response is rooted in early childhood experiences, it can be even more difficult to step back and ask the clarifying questions.

Cultural customs and norms are often part of our early childhood experience. As children we usually accept the way our parents or our people do things as the norm, the "right" way to do them. To the child, any other way appears wrong. The known way is the standard, and is obvious. As an adult, when you find yourself in circumstances where you are flooded with early childhood meanings and interpretation, knowing your cues becomes that much more helpful. It is a way to maintain your adult functioning, when your inner child is poised to take over.

For example, the police officer who steps out of his cruiser after pulling you over and says, "Where's the fire?" may obviously be telling you that you were speeding, that he is in a position of power over you, and that you had better start explaining yourself. In response to that "obvious" meaning, you can feel the hairs stand up on the back of your neck, and the goose bumps prickle as you turn red and hope he doesn't notice. You respond to the obvious threat and go into your defensive routine.

Or when you hear him say "Where's the fire?" you recognize a cultural custom, something that says we are all one people who share a history and a story and a great many things we know and do and say in common. "Where's the fire?" can be understood as the expression of a bond that we share, an attempt to lighten up an anxiety-producing situation. You recognize that this cop is obviously trying to make you feel better, trying to make a tense situation easier, and you respond with humor and positive regard. You are both adults in this ridiculous situation, each doing your job the best way you know how—no good guys, no bad guys, just life in America.

So when you feel that prickle on the back of your neck, take it as a cue: You are making meanings that will lead to your being defensive, and probably put you in your least resourceful child-state. It is to your benefit to check it out and learn whether the "obvious" is also true in the concrete world, or whether it is only your imagination intruding.

Your cues may come in the form of familiar internal dialogues. By internal dialogues, I am referring to your self-talk, the conversations you have with yourself that are not spoken aloud. For instance, when someone speaks to you in a manner you experience as a put-down, you may hear a voice inside saying, "You aren't going to let her get away with that, are you?" And you know that when you hear that voice chiding or taunting you, your defenses go up, your listening goes down, and you have embarked on a familiar routine. It may be a face-saving routine that draws from the Model I social virtue of support or respect. It may be an attacking routine that draws from the Model I social virtues of integrity and strength. It is probably not a routine that creates opportunities for collaboration or learning.

Although the opportunities for variety in our behavior are infinite, our ability to discern the opportunities is extremely limited. There are several ways by which we constrict our ability to respond. We are limited by the ways in which we think about the world. Our worldview and the designed blindness that sustains it serve to screen out information that either has no place on our map (and therefore makes no sense to us) or does not conform to our expectations. We are limited by our repertoire of behaviors, those we were taught and those we have devised and incorporated into our practice. We can only do what we know. We are limited by the social norms and conventions within which we function. The patterns we know, which sometimes work, and sometimes get us into serious trouble, are so well learned that they seem almost to have a life of their own. We may observe ourselves in the midst of an interaction which we know will be ineffective and hear in our self-talk, "Here we go again. Someone get me out of this!" But it is too late. The mistake was made and we have been trapped once again. How to interrupt our familiar patterns of interaction becomes a pressing concern when we are trying to learn.

Cues are essential. Feelings, words we say (such as "obviously"), and our internal dialogue are all potential carriers of cues that can help us identify the beginning of a familiar behavior pattern. These cues become the basic tools that help us recognize the ineffective routines and locate the situations in which we wish to implement this new behavior we are learning. By discovering an ineffective pattern and how it functions in our practice, we are empowered to invent an alternative. When we locate the cue that begins the routine, we know where to interrupt it, thereby learning to apply our new behavior over time.

We have seen how identifying cues such as thinking or saying that something is "obvious," engaging in particular kinds of self-talk, or experiencing negative feelings helps us discern when we have made the climb up the ladder of inference. They remind us to go back down and check our data. The cues that mark the start of a behavioral pattern may be located in our internal state, such as anxiety, a tightening in the stomach, anger, or pounding heart. The trigger may be in our internal dialogue, saying familiar things to ourselves such as, "Don't tell me what to do," or "That's not fair," which set us off and running. That trigger becomes a cue marking a place to stop and consider an alternative response.

Sometimes the cue surfaces in our external behavior. We may start speaking more loudly or more softly. We may withdraw eye contact, or assume a particular body posture that tells us that we are about to attack, cave in, withhold, or back away. We may hear ourselves saying things so familiar that we know we are engaged in a well-worn routine. Any one of these centers may be where the familiar behavior pattern begins. Therefore, identifying cues assists us not only in recognizing when we have begun to make inferences and attributions, but marks key points at which we could interrupt our behavior and introduce changes.

Mapping Our Theories-in-Use

In chapter 1 as we engaged in our three case studies of our colleagues, we observed that it is possible to map theories-in-use. Experiencing the map, we could recognize its power and possibility as an effective tool in predicting behavior. At least we could see that was true in the cases of others. How to discern and map your own theories-in-use is probably still a mystery. That puzzle is reasonable. I am asking you to become aware of something of which you are unaware. The phenomenon of designed blindness, coupled with the automatic nature of most of our behavior, makes such discernment of the theories that drive our action a significant challenge.

In the development of theories-in-use we have learned that what becomes important is the identification of the cues, because these were the choice-points. The cue allows us to locate the moment we are most likely to be able to interrupt the old pattern. At the moment the cue is triggered, we can choose to begin the old familiar routine, or to do something different. It is with the beginning of the sequence that we have the clearest option of doing something differently and changing the outcome.

Well-constructed theories-in-use are generic. Because these are behaviors we repeat in a variety of situations, a correctly identified cue becomes the effective key to unlocking the door to learning and applying new and more effective behaviors. Mapping them helps us to find the lock and fashion a key that fits our purpose.

Dyer's "Second Chance"

The Rev. Toby Dyer's theory-in-use, when she was confronting her staff about deciding one thing and then telling the personnel committee another was:

- When an event has meanings/implications that are obvious to me and not to others:
  Assume they do not understand what happened.
  Assume I do.

- Repeat over and over the events of the story, assuming that what is obvious to me will become so to them.

- Do not question my understanding or analysis.

- Do not inquire as to their understandings or analysis.

- Assume they have a covert agenda which is undiscussable.
  Experience myself as open, just, and honorable.
  Experience them as closed, unjust, and dishonorable.

- Feel betrayed, hurt, angry, isolated, and trapped.
  Become enraged.

- Publicly distance myself.
  Privately feel incompetent.

- Judge them as untrustworthy and give up collaboration.

What leaps out here is the notion that something is obvious. Dyer identified that as her most important clue. When she perceives something as obvious, her usual response is to assume that her perception is correct. Therefore, when others do not perceive the situation as she has, she assumes that their perception is in error, rather than questioning her own perception.

If she can interrupt herself at the point when others are not seeing what seemed obvious to her, and if she can consider that there may be valid alternative meanings, she moves herself out of this well-worn automatic response. She thus relieves herself from having to explain repeatedly that with which people do not agree. She instead moves into authentic engagement. All people can share their perceptions and the meanings they make of them. Caring about what others think and learning more effective behavior become Dyer's motives rather pushing her own point of view and winning others over to her position.

What is also contained in Dyer's theory-in-use is a "second chance" cue. That second cue is in her exterior behavior—when she hears herself repeating over and over the events of the story. Sometimes we are more attuned to our internal state or dialogue. Then the internal cues, a feeling or a thought, are the most helpful. But we may miss them. If we can also identify the next cue, external behavior, it gives us a second chance to stop and choose.

I say "choose" because I am not suggesting that people must discard all of their accustomed ways of being and responding. Those are hard-won skills. Most of the time those ways have served us well. I am not taking away any of the familiar tools, only offering new ones to add to the supply.

Consider the food processor, which can slice or chop foods in almost no time. No need to think, no time wasted. Much of our behavior is like the quick and simple action of the food processor. We act automatically without deliberation. This automatic pilot of ours can be very efficient. But sometimes the dish we are making requires that the vegetables be cut more precisely, in more uniform slices, or we need to achieve some more specific result than cannot be monitored effectively when something is whizzing around at great speed in an electric food processor. At those times it is more effective to get out a good sharp knife and make the exact cuts we want and need. The result ultimately will be less wasteful and more satisfying. So it is with this skill that begins by identifying cues. We are offering you ways to slow down the process so that you can interrupt it long enough to make choices. You can still choose the food processor, but if it isn't working, you can go back and retrieve the careful hand tool that requires more craft but will produce a more elegant result.

Dyer may not notice that she had assumed the "obvious" and that she is operating higher on the ladder of inference than will serve her well. If she can notice, however, that she is repeating again and again her understanding, and encountering resistance or distancing, she has the opportunity to consider that something obvious to her may not be obvious to others—may, in fact, be an error. She can still change her behavior at this point, cease her advocacy, and inquire. Discerning multiple cues of internal states, internal dialogues, and external behavior multiplies the opportunities for interrupting a sequence that is not working and redirecting it more productively.

Gellerd's Silence and Anger

For Gellerd the sequence is a little different. Gellerd's withholding of information was the beginning of the disastrous sequence, and her feelings followed. You can see this in the theory-in-use:

When I think something is important, withhold it.
When angry at not being heard because I haven't said what is important to me:
    Blame others for not hearing what I haven't said.
    Hold them responsible for my lack of participation.
    Give up, withdraw politely, and wonder what is wrong
    with them.

The beginning of Gellerd's theory-in-use is interesting. Within the setup of the routine she has cues in two different modes, each supporting the other. Note the pairing in the first line of a thought (something is important) and an external behavior (withholding). In a professional conference setting in which she customarily participates fully, both verbally and emotionally, if she notices that she is not speaking, she can take that silence as a cue to check if there is something she is withholding. If she discovers that she is withholding, she is then free to consider why, the probable consequences (intended or otherwise) of continuing to withhold, and whether to continue to do so.

This withholding was her first and most useful choice-point. There may have been a cue that preceded the withholding, however. For instance, Gellerd may notice that she was engaged in an internal dialogue about the topic. In the context of that awareness, she may also notice the intensity of the internal dialogue or her feelings in response to it. She could then identify how important she felt this matter was to her. In this case, the high level of intensity would have been a cue to her that she held it to be very important. At the point she notices that this dialogue is taking place inside her head and that it has not been shared, she again can decide whether to bring the information out into the conversation or withhold it. It is her choice, but now, with some understanding of the consequences of the decision, she can make an informed choice.

If Gellerd misses the initial cue, whether it is an external behavior or an internal dialogue, she too has a "second-chance" cue. It surfaces as her anger at not being heard—an internal state. When Gellerd finds herself becoming angry at not being heard, she can consider the possibility that she has not specifically told her listeners what she wanted them to hear. Before holding them responsible for their failing to hear, she can assume a greater responsibility for communicating.

For Gellerd, the problematic component which she replicates in various settings is the surprising (but not uncommon) expectation that somehow if the people around her really cared or really respected her, they would know what she is thinking—in other words, they would read her mind! (The common experience of an internal dialogue might go something like this: "If she really cared about me, she would know I can't stand [fill in the blank]"— but it is likely something you have never told her.) The experience of that particular anger is now a second-chance cue for Gellerd to be sure she has told her colleagues what they need to know. And if she chooses not to tell them, she is released from the rage that builds because they didn't know it.

Some of us are more aware of one mode of processing than another. It may be easier for you to pick up on internal state than on external behavior, or to notice internal dialogue before noticing internal feelings. To the extent that you can identify multiple cues, you will increase your opportunities to interrupt sequences you wish to change and multiply your likelihood of success.

Using Advocacy and Inquiry

You can break the escalating cycle of error and frustration by intentionally coupling inquiry to your advocacy. It is important to advocate for your position and your point of view. Everyone's wisdom and perception need to be brought to the table to maximize the information and ideas available. For the information, ideas, and perceptions to be useful, it is important that they be understood by the others at the table. When an understanding of that accumulated input is achieved, the participants can go on to examine the contributions for their strengths and weaknesses. All ideas would be improved by this process, as would the resulting decisions. Because the give-and-take of putting ideas forward and critically examining them produces the best result, the most productive behavior is advocacy coupled with inquiry. That inquiry would include asking about others' ideas and opinions, their meanings and intentions, generating as much DOD as possible. It would also include encouraging them to inquire about your own position, your reasoning, meanings, intentions, and to ask any other questions that would help them to understand and get as close to the DOD involved as possible.

You may not be able to do that at first. It is difficult, and most of us have trouble. So we recommend that you start small. A little inquiry can go a long way toward interrupting a quick slide into an unproductive behavior sequence or a faster-than-lightning run up the ladder of inference. Try noticing when you are advocating for something, and at the end of it add an inquiry. Just one. That simple change in behavior is a beginning, and you may be surprised by what you learn. You may feel a little awkward and inauthentic at first. After all, you really want to sell your idea. But stopping to inquire about someone else's perception may be enough to remind you that there are multiple possibilities. With that recognition, you are freed up to become open to new and creative possibilities without having given up the option of choosing your initial idea. What this will do for you is maximize your data, your information, your options, and your flexibility, thereby maximizing the likelihood that your choices will be sound and effective.

What's in Your Toolbox

We can use specific tools to interrupt the practices at which we have become skilled, the ineffective routines so well learned that we have called them our "skilled incompetence."

These tools include understanding and searching for the directly observable data within the presenting situation. The use of the ladder of inference can remind us that we have been operating out of untested inferences, attributions, and interpretations, and help return us to the directly observable data. The importance of inquiry in this process cannot be overstated. The more we inquire, the more likely we are to remain close to the data and further from error. Taking responsibility for maximizing available data on which sound decisions can be made entails maintaining an ongoing dialogue of advocacy combined with inquiry, ensuring that all ideas get out on the table and all conjectures can be tested.

We secure the best possible chance of being able to interrupt the old routines and produce the new desired behavior when the cues that appear at the beginning of the routine are identified and recognized. It is also possible to identify a second-phase cue that we are caught in a problematic routine, so that if the first trigger is released, a point of effective intervention is still accessible. Theories-in-use map our behavioral routines, and can be used to identify the triggering cues.

Finally, it is important to remember that all of these techniques are intended to be used in the service of Model II social virtues. To the extent that these tools are used by people who are building a bilateral agenda, attempting to generate the most information, and maximizing creativity and personal investment by all of the stakeholders, they are governed by Model II social virtues. In that circumstance, these techniques increase the likelihood that errors will be detected and corrected, that the gifts and insights brought to bear will be maximized and that overall effectiveness, both personal and collective, will be enhanced.

CHAPTER 4

Coaching For Change

We have been talking about becoming more effective religious profession-als, more skillful practitioners of our craft, and more faithful stewards of our call and charge. I have presented some conceptual frameworks in the form of the social virtues and their governing variables to help in that develop-ment. Out of that framework, I have given you some specific tools you can learn and apply to enable you to become more effective.

The Choice for Transformation

So far this is not unlike a lot of other "how to" clergy and professional handbooks (and there are many from which to choose). But there is one great difference in this approach. If you choose to embrace this process, to engage in the practices and reflection I am describing, you are making the choice to be transformed. You cannot do this work except by changing yourself. You cannot practice it without the consequence of being changed by it and by the others with whom you live and work.

The reason why your transformation is inevitable is that this model is a design for learning. It is about engaging in learning in real time, on-site, in the midst of your practice. It is about being open to the movement of the spirit that blows where it wills, and speaks through others as well as in our own head and heart. It is about being open to learning, which always in-cludes the risk or opportunity for transformation.

I believe that it is important for you to give your informed consent to participate in this learning. I want you to know the chances you take when you begin to practice Model II. However, it is difficult to convey the exact nature of that risk, since transformation does not mean the same thing for everyone.

A Surprising Transformation

Late spring marked the end of the academic year in our doctor of ministry program. Our teaching team had already submitted grades. A group of students who had made up the doctor of ministry seminar (in which we teach this material through the use of case studies) asked to have a meeting with the teaching team and the academic dean. The meeting was held. There was tension when we walked into the room. The students were braced for a confrontation. In our presence, they voiced their complaint to the dean. They did not think that they should have been required to take the course. It wasn't fair. The dean asked them if they had learned anything during the year. "Yes," they all agreed, and most went on to say that they had learned more in that course than they had ever learned in any course in their lives. "So what is the problem?" the dean asked perplexedly. "We were transformed!" they answered.

More inquiry on the part of the dean revealed that they expected that they should be able to study for an academic degree, learn what was necessary, and become a doctor of ministry, without being changed. Academic learning, in their understanding, was about neither change nor personal transformation. It was only about adding facts to their knowledge base. That is not our understanding. Authentic learning, in our experience, changes the learner. The learner's world expands, discernment is sharpened, some ideas are given up, and others are taken in. Perspectives of others that one could not have generated out of one's own personal story become a part of the learner's new reality. As those things happen, the learner's self is transformed.

Although I believe that transformation occurs even in an educational process focused merely on the cognitive aspects of learning, I intend the learner to change as a result of the suggestions and opportunities I am offering. What makes this opportunity particularly challenging, even exhilarating, is that I am offering you a different way to understand your goals, your outcomes, and your way of being in the world.

Double-Loop Learning

I am not only asking you to change the way you behave so that you might more effectively achieve your goals; I am asking you to consider whether your present goals are the ones you want to pursue. Are they worthy? How do you know that? In other words, I am asking you to engage in "double-loop learning," the kind of learning in which you ask questions not only about the way you are doing something but about why you are doing it. It is as though you are doubling back, going beyond the presenting question, to the first question that precedes it.

I am asking you to step back from your practice and look at yourself as someone else might look at you. And then I want you to ask "Why?" "Why did I do that?" "What was I thinking?" "What was I feeling or intending? What was I concealing?" "Whom was I serving?" "What values and purposes was I serving?" "Ought they be served?" I am raising more than the matter of how you can do something better—namely, the question of whether you should be doing it at all.

These are hard questions because they raise feelings of discomfort that often would seem simpler to avoid. It is uncomfortable to call into question goals and practices that we have taken for granted and assumed as foundational to who we are or what we do. Asking double-loop questions can be disorienting, as it causes us to distinguish between what is actually an unchangeable given, and what exists because we have accepted it or allowed it to be so. Often we are surprised when we recognize that something we accepted as "always being that way" was not always that way, or does not need to be so. The double-loop questions are hard to craft because they require you to do something you may not yet be accustomed to doing. Robert Kegan calls the ability to raise double-loop questions and engage in double-loop learning "fourth-order thinking." Kegan believes thinking at the fourth order is essential for functioning well in today's world and that many of us do not know how to do it.

Most of us are able to function as a members of society, knowing its norms, its lore, its meanings and expectations. Being able to understand the society into which we have been well socialized is called "third-order thinking," But this kind of thinking has limitations that create barriers to further learning. Third-order thinking "is not able to reflect critically on that into which it is being socialized. It is responsible to socialization, not responsible for it."[1]

I am inviting you into fourth-order thinking, to detect the cultural air you breathe and to determine if it is good or toxic. I am asking you not only to become effective, but to become responsible—responsible for the goals (and gods) you have chosen to serve.

Questioning the Rules

Here is an example of what we mean by "double-loop learning." Consider a thermostat. A thermostat is set at a particular temperature—for instance, 68 degrees Fahrenheit. An effective thermostat maintains that temperature, continually adjusting the heat output to ensure that the temperature remains at 68. That thermostat is a single-loop learner.

There is, however, an outside force and an outside intelligence that can objectively survey the scene and determine whether 68 is an appropriate setting. If the room is going to be used for an exercise class, 62 might be better. If the room will be home to a hospice patient, 74 degrees might be more appropriate.

When we step back and ask why the thermostat is set as it is, and then go further and ask if that is an appropriate setting, we are engaging in double-loop learning and thinking in the fourth order. From the fourth-order position, the answer "We've always done it that way" will just not do. Neither will "68 degrees Fahrenheit is the correct setting." Fourth-order thinking can always ask "Why?" or "Why not?"

Fourth-order thinking is hard not only because it is often difficult to construct the questions. It is hard because thinking in the fourth order carries with it a recognition of responsibility. Once we have reframed the questions, we have also reframed our responsibility and know that it is ours. We choose the goals we serve.

Resisting the move into fourth-order thinking means avoiding the knowledge that our social order and the myriad other contexts in which we function are human constructions. They are constructions which we support and perpetuate as participants. They are also subject to deconstruction or correction.

For example, there was a time in the world when slavery was considered by most a universal human condition. We can find that assumption running through the Bible, both in Hebrew Scripture and Christian Scripture. Third-order thinkers might have been troubled by the suffering slavery engendered, and some of them might have tried to design ways to make slavery more humane. It took fourth-order thinkers to challenge the concept of slavery and the belief that it was inevitable.

Third-order thinking knows the rules but does not accept responsibility for creating or critiquing them. That level of thinking is developmentally appropriate and acceptable for the adolescent, but it is unacceptable to stay in that place through adulthood. We refuse the invitation to grow in wisdom and faithfulness when we resist knowing what can be known. Our development is stunted. By turning our backs on the growth process, we may decline to learn the skills needed to be responsible selves. Choosing ignorance, however, does not abrogate our responsibility.

We have witnessed the dilemma evoked for people by this ethical imperative to know what can be known. It requires actively making decisions about our behavior. In recent times conflict erupted between that ethical imperative and the authority of the state. Under the rule of the Third Reich only third-order thinking was permitted. Ultimately the Nazis were not relieved of the responsibility incurred by living in the third-order thinking that allowed them simply to follow orders. Neither are we relieved. In the final accounting we are responsible for the goals (and gods) we choose to serve. The tools we are providing will help you to ask those fourth-order questions, meet the ethical challenge, and become authentically responsible selves.

When Jesus cured the man who had been blind from birth, enabling the man to see, he was questioned by those who did not understand.

"Surely we are not blind, are we?" they asked. And Jesus said to them, "If you were blind, you would not have sin. But now that you say, 'We see,' your sin remains" [John 9:40-41].

What Jesus is talking about is becoming responsible selves. The blindness that comes with birth, the blindness that results from authentic ignorance and unknowing, is not sin. For that we are not culpable. However, for those things that are within our power of knowing and seeing, for those things that could be in our awareness and to which we have turned a blind eye, we are responsible.

Once we have become adults, once we have claimed to be able to see, we are then responsible for our designed blindness, and to the extent that we maintain and continue to foster our unawareness of it, we sin. We sin not only because we do that which we ought not do; we sin because we could have known it, we could have seen, and we chose otherwise.

Coaching for Growth

How do we make those developmental leaps, or even the small incremental steps? If we are sinning and cannot maintain awareness of it, how can we correct ourselves? If we cannot conceive of the fourth-order questions because we mistakenly assume that the status quo is necessary or permanent, how do we grasp that there is another way? We have found it helpful to think in terms of coaching.

In the world of athletic training, the coach stands apart and watches the developing athlete. The coach may not even be as good an athlete as the one being trained. But the coach is good at giving athletes the information they need in forms they can use. The coach provides feedback to athletes, advising them what it appears they need to increase strength, gain precision, develop new strategies, or simply practice more. The coach may help athletes accurately assess their performance and the related consequences. The coach gives clear, usable feedback. The coach does not do the work. It is not possible for anyone but the athlete to incorporate the new perceptions and understandings, and to customize the learnings so that they may be integrated into his or her own athletic practice.

The movement from third order to fourth order must happen over time. There is a growth process within third-order thinking that prepares us to make the step into fourth-order thinking and responsibility. We cannot be pushed or carried over by someone else. We cannot grow at the pace others might wish. We must do it in our own self-generated, self-motivated way. And often we need help. Effective coaching recognizes the role and the limits of the one who would help.

Model II Social Virtues

Among the critical tools to help you move in the direction of developed fourth-order thinking are the Model II social virtues. They will allow you more freedom to learn, to listen, and to adjust. For example, you can change your way of understanding virtue, of understanding what it means to support and respect others. What you thought was strength you may now recognize as brittleness or stubbornness. With the new Model II understanding of strength and integrity, you may perceive dimensions of those qualities you still need to develop. You are challenged both to advocate and authentically to encourage others to confront you with their inquiry. You may have never tried being vulnerable in a situation of stress while not feeling threatened. Learning how to use advocacy and inquiry to that end takes practice.

You now ask what effective and appropriate leadership might be. You discover an alternative to the common polarities of "authoritative" leadership or "client-centered" (servant) leadership. You now know about the alternative of bilateral, collaborative leadership. The leader neither abdicates nor controls, but engages in a mutual learning process from which the directions for leadership emerge.

How Learning Comes About

All this change can happen, albeit it slowly, in bits and pieces. We need insight and time to internalize and act on the altered perceptions. It is important to understand that transformational learning is not necessarily gradual learning. Often there is a period when the old ways are being challenged and the practitioner observes from a distance. Then something happens for the practitioner that allows him or her to grasp the nature of the challenge and the new insights and opportunities it offers. Something "clicks." Suddenly the old way does not feel as comfortable or as trustworthy as it once did. It is flawed. But the new way is only an inkling and a promise. Caught between the exposure of error in what you know, and the uncertainty about how to correct it, you begin to feel incompetent. You are confused, periodically visited by moments of clarity and flashes of understanding. Like epiphanies, they may be difficult to hold onto.

When you take on the active role of learner, you will periodically have these disconcerting experiences. Usually such experiences are followed by plateau periods, in which the learnings are integrated. You are crafting a new worldview and self-understanding. You may well reconfigure your espoused theories as well as your theories-in-use in response to the learnings.

Incorporating Your Learning

The new behaviors need to be incorporated into your practice. It will take time for them to become comfortable parts of your repertoire. Your learning curve will include great strides forward, occasional steps back, and resting places while you test and internalize what has been newly learned. A slow, self-paced process will be more effective than trying to rush through it.

Remember, you became very skillful at what you presently do—the things that work and the things that don't—because you spent years practicing and honing those skills. It is understandably disconcerting to consider relinquishing some skills in the hope of finding something better. I am not asking you to do that. I encourage you to keep all of the tools and techniques you have mastered in your professional toolbox. There may well be times when it is appropriate to use them. What you can do is add tools to your repertoire, and develop the skill base that will help you to use them.

The wise proverb reminds us, "If all you have is a hammer, the whole world looks like a nail." However, if you discard your hammer when someone gives you a screwdriver, then "all the world looks like a screw." That is not really helpful either. If you have spent your professional life hammering and someone gives you a screwdriver, you need to learn how to use the screwdriver. When we bang on a screw with a screwdriver, we are using the right tool in the right situation, but we are still not releasing the tool's useful potential. When we are first given a screwdriver, we must learn how to press and twist, a new technique, uncomfortable and slow compared to the familiar rapid response we get when we use the hammer to hit a nail. It is difficult to take up behavior that is predictably awkward (as learning most new skills is) when what we already know comes naturally.

Beginning the Change

The most helpful and retrievable way to begin to change is to identify the first cues that elicit the behavior you wish to alter. Something triggers the routine, and, like an automatic pilot, you put your ineffective theory-in-use into action. That cue is important to identify, because it will enable you to choose a new behavior and interrupt the routine. That cue, as we learned, can be identified in your internal state (feelings), internal dialogue (self-talk), or external behavior (what you do).

When you identify the beginning of an ineffective routine, you do more than simply note the cue. Everything connected with the cue will change as you change your understanding of its meaning. Previously, the "irresponsible self" would not have even acknowledged the cue, let alone the resulting behavior. Using designed blindness with the speed and skill of an expert, the previously unaware self would place the responsibility and causation outside the self. You would have said, or thought, "He made me mad." "I couldn't help it." "She humiliated me." "I felt trapped." By avoiding our responsibility for the creation of problems, we lose our power to correct them. What had been a skill designed for our safety and protection (blindness) becomes a barrier. Without the power of correction we cannot create safety.

These cues function to trigger a behavior. Once that routine begins, we feel compelled to follow it to completion out of a belief that no alternative exists. Just to stop and recognize that you can choose is to change your world, beginning the move into fourth-order thinking. Even more change happens with that recognition. Your internal state, internal dialogue, and external behavior are intimately and undeniably connected to each other. When you change one, you change the others. You dismiss or disregard one function over another at your peril.

Levels of Change

You live and work within the context of many related systems operating on different levels. The intrapersonal level, made up of your own inner parts, is but one of them. The family, other institutions, and social structures are all systems in which we participate. Systems function in similar ways regardless of their context. Using one system, such as the body, to talk about another system, such as the church, is a powerful teaching tools. Using such illustrative metaphors helps people get unstuck from their particular position so they can understand their proper relationship to the whole.

The Apostle Paul taught the people of the church at Corinth:

> If the whole body were an eye, where would the hearing be? If the whole body were hearing, where would the sense of smell be? But as it is, God arranged the members in the body, each one of them, as he chose. If all were a single member, where would the body be? As it is, there are many members, yet one body. . . . there may be no dissension within the body, but the members may have the same care for one another. If one member suffers, all suffer together with it; if one member is honored, all the members rejoice together with it [1 Cor. 12:14, 17-20, 25-26].

What Paul describes happening in the physical body is true also on both the intrapersonal and interpersonal levels. As you change the way in which you think about others, you change the ways you behave with them. Changing the ways you behave with them alters the ways in which they interact with and respond to you. Helping the positive changes emerge in the people and institutions we serve is the purpose and the premise of becoming an effective practitioner of ministry.

The one body (system) about which Paul is speaking is the faith community. But we know that the truth about the interrelatedness of systemic components is true for the larger communities to which we belong—towns, cities, nations, continents. Each member is affected by the well-being of the other, and each is enhanced to the extent that all members are empowered to bring their gifts and skills to the table.

Paul coaches and admonishes the church to include all the people in their processes of church governance, maintenance, and discernment. To leave any out is to lose the benefit of their gifts, and reveals a lack of understanding of God's intent. People are created differently, that they might work together for mutual enhancement. From this we understand that bilateral discernment, planning, and evaluation are not only effective; they are encouraged by Scripture. But what Paul says about community applies to us individually as well. It is not by chance that Paul can turn to the body as a metaphor for the way in which whole systems work, displaying properties and capacities that are greater than any of the parts alone or even their sum. He appeals to our own experiences as selves. We know "from inside" that when one part of us changes, other parts change as well.

Systemic Change

The self is a system that processes what is going on and determines actions to be taken. We have identified three processing modes you use: internal state (feeling), internal processing (thinking), and external behavior.[1] You feel something; you talk to yourself about it; you do (or say) something, which leads you to feel something, to talk to yourself about it, to do something (or refrain from doing it—which is also an action decision).

The order for each of us may vary. What doesn't vary is that changing the way you think will change the way you feel and will change the conversations you have with yourself inside your head. It does not matter in which mode you locate your cue. If you miss picking up the cue at the beginning of your routine, you may get a second chance with a later cue that you recognize as part of your familiar pattern. Once you have changed something about the way you process, think about, or understand what is going on around you and the choices you have, *everything* changes. And when that happens, you will *feel* transformed—and you *will* be.

How We Generate Feelings

Once you become more aware of the internal processes that generate your routines, your way of relating to and understanding your feelings will change. After years of culturally encouraged stoicism in which people denied or repressed their feelings, the 1960s in America produced an awakening to the life of feelings and emotions. There was much celebration and much exploration, for there was so much to learn. Instead of denying feelings, we were taught and regularly reminded, as individuals and as counselors, that feelings were facts. We were admonished to accept people's feelings, including our own. We were cautioned that feelings were not to be judged by the categories of right and wrong, which are appropriately applied to behavior. There is wisdom in these warnings, but they fall short, and many of us have been caught in the frustration of trying to accept people's feelings when those feelings appear to us to be inappropriate responses.

The more accurate and complicated truth is that although feelings are not right and wrong in the ethical (deontological) sense, they can be in error. Our feelings are generated in response to meanings we make of the world around us and what is going on. If a dog is running toward us and the meaning we make is that it is a friendly dog, perhaps our neighbor's pooch running up to say hello, we will greet it warmly, and we will feel affection. If, on the other hand, the meaning we make is that we are in danger, that the dog running toward us might hurt us, our response is defensive, and we will feel fear or anxiety.

Feelings are facts, but they are facts about how we make meaning of and respond to situations. Those foundational meanings *could* be in error, thus generating inappropriate and ultimately unhelpful responses. If we assume that all dogs are dangerous, we have lost out on the opportunity for the warm affectionate feelings that positive interactions with dogs can generate. If we assume all dogs are friendly, we could easily put ourselves in harm's way and be injured.

It is not enough to trust our feelings, because feelings grow out of reasoning processes. These processes are so fast that we often hardly know they happened. Dog-fear, or dog-affection. We so often experience the feeling and the perception simultaneously that we are unaware of the reasoning process that generated the emotion. But it was there.

Checking Feelings for Accuracy

When we respond to a tone in someone's voice, for instance, either positively or negatively, or when we hear what is said as criticism rather than as assistance, it is because we have gone through a reasoning process and ascribed a meaning to what we have heard. And that process could be flawed, generating errors. Consequently the feeling with which we respond might be in error, although it is a fact and as such neither right or wrong.

Engaging in Model II social virtues within our own minds as well as in interpersonal relations opens up the possibility of discovering those errors. When we are having strong emotional responses, we can check out whether we have climbed up high on the ladder of inference. If we are indeed up there, functioning with very little metaphorical "air," it is time to climb back down to terra firma, where we can retrieve the life-sustaining reality of directly observable data.

We discover that we can control our feelings, rather than having them control us. We can test, check, and modify our feelings and responses to people and the world around us from accurate observation. We can correct our perceptions, thus increasing the relevancy, propriety, and helpfulness of what we do. This ability is liberating and transforming. As with all liberty, there is a price. Freedom and responsibility are sides of the same coin. They always have been.

It is difficult to know when you are high up the ladder of inference. We make meanings so rapidly that the process of climbing the ladder is often outside our awareness. Like the kitten caught in the high branches of a tree, we need coaching to help get us back down. We need others to tell us what they see about us that we cannot see. We need to hear others who tell us that what we heard is not what they meant. We need those who will offer additional correctives as well, who will coach us into stepping back and asking the fourth-order questions that enable us to check our compass bearing and adjust our course.

Prophetic Voices from the Fourth Level

We need those who can speak their truth in faithfulness and love. So it was that the prophets thundered, coaxed, and cajoled their beloved people. The prophets, from Amos to Isaiah, took the people back to the basic questions, reminded them of the covenant and of the relationship with God it was meant to sustain and fulfill. With varying degrees of skill and success, they spoke to the people about fourth-order concerns.

Some people understood. We know that because there were those who preserved the prophetic challenges by recording and retelling them within the community and down the generations. Later people also recognized the wisdom, choosing to include the prophets' teaching words within the canon. Year after year we read these texts as part of our religious tradition's disciplines. We are challenged by the prophets. As we engage the texts, we know that it has always been difficult for the people to understand. We can infer the difficulty people have long experienced when engaging the prophets by looking at disciplines and practices within our religious traditions. Both the Jewish and Christian lectionaries insist on the faithful experiencing that prophetic encounter, year after year, generation after generation.

Amos roars at a people who are trapped in their third-order thinking.

I hate, I despise your festivals, and I take no delight in your
solemn assemblies;
Even though you offer me your burnt offerings and grain
offerings,
    I will not accept them;
And the offerings of well-being of your fatted animals
    I will not look upon.
Take away from me the noise of your songs,
    I will not listen to the melody of your harps.
But let justice roll down like waters,
    And righteousness like an ever-flowing stream
            [Amos 5:21-24, emphasis added].

Third-order thinking allowed the people to follow the rites and rituals without attending to the overarching meanings and reasons for them. They thought they knew what God required, but they had only comprehended part of the covenant. God requires justice and kindness, as well as a humility in walking in the ways that are holy (Micah 6:8). The rituals signify obedience. They signify the intention of the supplicant to walk humbly with God. But they are intended to be symbolic of a larger intention to obey God. The people had forgotten, or had become blind to, the purpose of their covenant: justice, justice, justice, and kindness.

The rituals became ends in themselves. And God roared. Third-order thinkers scratched their heads. Fourth-order thinkers got it. Many, many people over thousands of years have found in Amos the coaching words they needed to hear to make the transition from one order of thinking to the next. It was not that the rituals were bad. It was not that the rituals were being criticized. The rituals, when properly observed, served fourth-order goals. When the faithful performed the required rituals within the context of a commitment to justice and kindness (Micah 6:8), their hearts would open to all who were in their care and God's embrace.

The ritual was good practice if it served as a vehicle and not as a substitute for the larger goal. Fourth-order thinkers knew that, and there have been fourth-order thinkers in every generation. In the early days of our people, some of them became our prophets, coaching us, and some of them became our scribes, writing down and recording what our prophets had to say to us. Some of them became our religious leaders, continually interpreting the rituals and traditions, so that the people might remember the God they served. We the clergy, shaping a new century, inherit that charge of interpreting and that responsibility of pointing beyond the rites and rituals to the heart of God.

Pastors as Coaches

Often the role of the effective clergy practitioner, as a pastor or as an administrator, is to be a coach. The changes we seek are not only for ourselves. We enable people to develop in faith and, we hope, to achieve the capacity for fourth-order thinking. We desire that our congregants as well our staff become more competent and thus more effective in putting their faith into practice. We hope to help create more faithful communities. The question is how.

Roaring, ranting, and raving, the tradition reveals, don't really work, not consistently, not well. Amos tried. Amos told the people the fourth-order reasons for God's displeasure. But he didn't offer them the reasoning steps that would help them become fourth-order knowers.

Amos didn't teach them how, in the course of performing mandated rituals, to step back and ask why. "Why does God want us to do this? What is the higher purpose it is designed to serve? Is this a symbol of something, or is it the thing itself? If it is a symbol, then what does it point to and symbolize?" And finally, "Is it effective?"

Because he didn't teach them the skills, they did not know how to do the religious reflection required and were continuously at risk of evoking God's displeasure. They needed to learn the steps. They needed more than one example, so they could understand that his concern was not about this one single event. They needed more than chastisement. They needed coaching. So do we, the descendants, who stand on the shoulders of these brave and bold ancestors, repeating their mistakes.

God tries again and again, sending the message, and offering the coaching in different ways, that more of us might be helped to understand and grow. From the early prophet Amos, we heard the thundering wake-up call. Much later the prophet Isaiah spoke to us, a little differently, this time with more coaching.

Is such the fast that I choose,
    a day to humble oneself?
Is it to bow down like the head of a bulrush,
    and to lie in sackcloth and ashes?
Will you call this a fast,
    a day acceptable to the Lord?
Is not this the fast that I choose:
    To loose the bonds of injustice,
    To undo the thongs of the yoke,
To let the oppressed go free,
    And to break every yoke?
Is it not to share your bread with the hungry
    And bring the homeless poor into your house;
When you see the naked, to cover them,
    And not hide yourself from your own kin?
Then your light shall break forth like the dawn [Isa. 58:5-8].

Isaiah, another prophet speaking to another generation, continued the familiar theme. He wanted the people to understand what they were doing from the perspective of fourth-order thinking. But his approach was a little different.

Isaiah tried inquiry. While not full, open-ended inquiry, in that he was not in an interactive dialogue, he posed the issue to the people as a question. He wanted them to think. What he said must have been startling to many of them. Their first response may well have been confusion. After all, had they not understood that God required fasting as a religious discipline? And did not fasting often leave one fatigued, tired, and in the presence of God in worship feeling a little weak, a bit humbled, with one's head bent down like a bulrush?

So when the prophet asked, "Will you call this fast a day acceptable to the Lord?" they might have scratched their heads. In that moment of confusion, unsure of what they knew, their attention was engaged. Once they were listening, Isaiah reframed the situation, naming the fast by its purpose rather than by its form.

He didn't suggest that they ought not fast. He tried to offer them an alternative way of understanding what it means to be obedient to God. He suggested that the form of the fast should reflect its higher meaning and purpose. Coaching the people, Isaiah nudged them (and hopefully us) a little closer to fourth-order thinking and fourth-order living. Isaiah offered a lesson in discernment as well as practice.

Becoming a Coach

If you as a religious leader can function as coach, moving people along into fourth-order thinking, your job will be a whole lot easier. You also will find that in the process your capacity to be faithful, to listen and think clearly, to step back and practice faithful discernment will be enhanced.

The quality of personal and corporate thinking in your community will improve. So will the solutions produced and the outcomes realized. As your community learns to ask questions about the meanings and intentions of decisions, you develop an organizational learning loop. Each outcome becomes the subject of evaluation, producing new questions and discoveries. Outcomes then neither succeed nor fail. Outcomes are simply stopping points for reflection and discernment through which learning happens and improved ideas and processed are developed. When people learn to ask those questions in the organizational setting, and discover the value of such questions, they can transport that skill into other areas of their lives.

Dyer: Constructing a Solution

We can see how developing these learning skills yields a more effective professional practice by revisiting Toby Dyer. We remember that Dyer is the pastor of a church with a fairly large staff. Many of her difficulties related to increasing her effectiveness in management. After Dyer had presented the earlier case, she decided to be more intentional in bringing her Model II values into practice. A situation in her ministry provided just such a challenge. She was confronted with an inconsistency in her behavior, which enabled her to ask some of the double-loop questions we are encouraging. It was an unfolding process.

Dyer, in a meeting of the clergy team, was discussing how to empower all the full-time staff. In this setting the clergy team of four met weekly to discuss their ministries and the well-being of the church. The functioning of staff was often on the team's agenda. In response to a concern raised by one of the group, Dyer thought that a way to increase ownership of staff issues and decisions, and to enhance staff cooperation, was to alter the existing practice of her chairing the weekly staff meetings. She suggested instead changing to a rotating chair. She asked team members for their opinions.

The four members of the clergy team all thought that would be a good practice. They would be willing to take a turn as chair. At the next weekly meeting of the full-time staff Dyer told the gathering (consisting of the administrator, the director of music, the senior custodian, and the clergy team) that the clergy team had heard them express frustration with how things were often decided either by lay leaders or by the ministers, without consulting them. Work about which they had not been consulted was dumped on them. Sometimes expectations were unrealistic. Sometimes they knew more about the issue or problem than did the people who decided. Dyer and the other ministers wanted the rest of the full-time staff to feel consulted and part of the decision-making process. To open up the process and make it more collaborative, she wanted the chair of the weekly staff meetings to rotate. Each person would take a turn organizing the agenda and chairing the meeting.

Much to her shock and chagrin, the director of music refused. The administrator refused. The head custodian refused. The only ones willing were the three who had been at the original meeting at which the idea was generated.

Dyer realized she had encountered a dilemma: One cannot *unilaterally* create a *bilateral* strategy. The intention of the strategy was to increase the staff's personal ownership and sense of empowerment. Ironically, they exercised that agency and tested the authenticity of her stated intention by refusing the opportunity extended.

"That's your job," the director of music said. "It's too much work," the administrator said. "I don't do that; it's not my job," the head custodian said.

Dyer felt sorely tempted to respond like the Little Red Hen in the fable and say, "All right then, I'll do it myself." But she was able to step back and ask herself why she had made the original proposal.

Her intention for the proposed change was to increase the participants' sense of ownership of these meetings and of personal efficacy. All in the room had identified what they needed to do or not do to feel empowered and respected in their roles. Reconstructing her reasoning and remembering the goal, which she still believed to be valid, this is what she did.

DYER: I hear your disagreement, and respect your need to protect your time and choose which things you will take on. I hadn't realized that some of you would experience chairing our meeting as stressful extra work. I suggested this because everyone here is important and has a critical and unique role to play. This had seemed a way of acknowledging that and allowing each of you to help shape what we do. I didn't hear anyone say that was a bad idea or a goal you objected to. Am I getting this right? *[There are nods around the room.]* I only heard that some of you do not want to chair the meeting; doing so would not accomplish those positive things but rather would make you feel uncomfortable and maybe even resentful. Is that right? *[The dissenting parties nod or express assent.]*

DYER: However, I am also aware that J, P, and M *[the clergy team]* have expressed a willingness and interest in chairing the meetings. It would give them that feeling of participation and investment. Is that still so?

J, P, and M: Yes.

DYER: In that case, I propose that those people who want to participate in the rotation of the role of chair be able to do so, and those who would rather not, be free to decline. *[All except the director of music agree. To Dyer those in the room look as though they have become more relaxed.]*

MUSIC DIRECTOR: I still think it is your job. You are the senior minister! That means that you are supposed to be in charge.

DYER: In some ways I am. I am responsible for how the staff works together. So since you feel comfortable with me being in charge, and I feel comfortable sharing the chair, what I will do as the person in charge is allow us to try this new system for the next couple of months. That will give each of the people who volunteered two opportunities to chair. Then we can all evaluate it together, and make any changes which we think will help us collaborate and cooperate as staff. Is that OK? *[Everyone agrees, a date is scheduled for the evaluation, and the process goes forward.]*

What we see in this exchange is Dyer's sharing of her reasoning process, a continual checking out of perceptions and inferences made on the basis of the directly observable data, and a looping back to the original premise of moving to a more participatory and consultative staff relationship, putting it forward for confirmation or rejection.

By continually checking against the higher intention that the strategy was intended to serve, rather getting caught in advocating for a position as if that were the goal itself, Dyer was able to construct a solution that was congruent with the higher goal.

Those who wanted to participate and those who didn't were each able to experience personal causality and ownership of the staff meeting and its structure, even though the shape it took was not one any of them had anticipated before coming to the meeting.

Within this case is a lesson you can routinely apply in your own setting. Check the rules, practices, or "laws" (written or unwritten), not only for what they say, but for the intention they were created to serve. If the way that people are accustomed to doing something is creating a problem, ask what purpose the behavior was intended to serve. Committees may be dysfunctional for a variety of reasons. One reason that is seldom considered is that the committee no longer serves a useful or needed function. Rather than struggling to "fix" a committee that isn't working, first ask the question, "Why is the committee here?" Then, "Is that still necessary?"

Challenging an Outworn Practice

The board of directors of a denominationally connected retirement home met once a month. At the beginning of the meeting the executive director and the director of nursing gave their reports. They were then excused from the meeting. When the home hired a chaplain, he began attending board meetings as well. He too would be excused after his report. That troubled him. When he asked a few people the purpose of excusing the staff, they said that was how it had always been done and that was how the board was comfortable.

After this brief research, when the chaplain was told he could leave at the next board meeting, he said, "Thank you, but I'd like to stay." The board was stunned, but could think of no reason to exclude him. During the course of the next few months he observed the board spending much time discussing matters about which they had little information. The information was readily available in the person of the director and the director of nursing. When it was suggested that the board could call them back in to get the information, board members declined, believing that the directors were too busy.

In later discussion with the two directors the chaplain learned that they were not too busy. They did remember that years ago when the home had been in difficult financial straits, the home was not fully staffed. In those days, before these two had been hired, it was true that the directors could not afford the time for board meetings because they were carrying other responsibilities. When the directors realized that they were not included in the meetings because many years ago in a different situation the practice was unworkable, they started to think differently. They began to think about what it would be like to understand the reasoning of the board on decisions that the executive director and the director of nursing had to implement. They thought about the possibility of having input to these decisions. They became excited.

At the next board meeting they told the board they wished to remain too. A new dynamic was created appropriate to the new situation, and a working partnership between the board and the staff was forged. An unexpected consequence of this shift: It was so successful that eventually the residents were invited to select one of their number to sit in on board meetings so that every stakeholder was represented at the sessions. Because questions were asked about the purpose of the board and what it needed to make its best decisions, new strategies were devised and effectiveness was increased.

One way to engage in discerning the value of particular laws, rules, or practices is to ask, "Why are we doing that?" Another way to push for the deeper question is to ask, "What would happen if we didn't do it that way?"

That check is one way to begin asking double-loop questions and initiate double-loop learning for yourself and others.

Being Open to Inquiry

Another axiom helped Dyer maintain her fourth-order thinking, while holding herself open and accountable. It is a valuable tool, almost like an insurance policy, when designing interventions:

Never use a strategy you are unwilling to discuss.

Dyer's willingness to discuss her intention and her strategy rendered her behavior congruent with her thoughts and feelings, as well as congruent with her tone and her presentation. She was capable of tolerating inquiry with minimal defensiveness. The staff was more effective as a team and more often solved problems creatively.

This is not how we are accustomed to working. Many practitioners spend a great deal of time before such a meeting thinking, strategizing, and sometimes even consulting with friends and colleagues. We bring to those sessions our private internal processing or the results of our consultations with others. We work with our perceptions, inferences, meanings, and attributions. Usually we do not have much directly observable data. We hardly notice its absence, and often neither do our friends or colleagues. Plans are based on undetected error.

We are asking you to consult directly observable hard data as you attempt to understand reality. In the long span of human history this is a relatively new concept. Prior to the rise of empirical science at the turn of the previous millennium, the sages of the day attempted to achieve understanding and to decipher conundrums through the process of reason alone. The issues and concerns were formulated as questions, and ideas were explored through the fire and discipline of abstract logic, but not through the fire of testing the data.

The Turn to Data

It is worth looking for a moment at one conundrum that had gripped the intellectual community from the time of the philosopher Aristotle to the era of mathematicians Euclid and Ptolemy. It is interesting because it reveals how blindness functioned to create error in yet another and distant situation. It is valuable because it illustrates what creativity and learning become possible when we climb down the ladder of inference and confront the data of reality.

The hero of our story is Abu Ali al-Hassan Ibn-al-Haytham, born in what is now Iraq in 965 C.E. Against all cultural norms and expectations Ibn-al-Haytham interrupted a pattern of self-sealed single-loop disagreement between the great thinkers who held conflicting theories about how the eye functioned. The argument had been going on for 800 years.

The question as posed was whether the source of light came from outside and penetrated the eye, or whether the source of light was the eye itself, which shone upon the objects of its vision. There were those who sided with Euclid, Ptolemy and the mathematicians who through their discipline demonstrated (and, they believed, "proved") that light traveled from the eye directly to the observed object. Aristotle and the atomists proved within their theoretical discipline that light traveled from the object into the eye.

Each had neat and tidy theories. Each theory was internally consistent. There was no bridge between them and no way to arbitrate, since each was working within self-sealed loops and asking only single-loop questions. Our hero, Ibn-al-Haytham, made an observation. He invited others to make it as well. It was a simple experiment. He suggested that the people stare at the sun. When they tried, they could do so only for a limited period of time. Eventually, the light from the sun burned the eye, and they had to stop. Therefore, he suggested, theory or no theory, it was clear that the light traveled from the outside in, penetrating the eye.

Subtly, but profoundly, Ibn al-Haytham introduced a revolution in human development by changing our perceptions. By suggesting that the answer to the question could be tested in the embodied world of concrete things and lived experience, he brought awareness of the value of material culture into the practice of disciplined thought. Whereas abstract thinking had previously been considered sufficient, he introduced the concept of physical data. It was not sufficient for theories to work within the confines of a discrete system. Explanatory theories needed to be confirmed or proved wrong by data. All of our technological achievements and the development of further understanding of human behavior have Ibn al-Haytham's innovative contribution as their foundational cornerstone. In its refined form we know it as the scientific method. It shaped a millennium.[2]

Science today is not just a matter of thinking one's way into truth, but a way of analyzing and encountering concrete reality. We may find it amazing that what is obvious to us now had such a recent beginning. Even more amazing is that there are ways in which we are still more like Euclid and Aristotle than we are like Ibn al-Haytham.

Crossing the Line to Fourth-Order Thinking

In a class at Harvard's Graduate School of Education in the 1980s Chris Argyris was lecturing. In the previous class he had discussed Model I, and at this point in the class he was finishing his explanation of Model II. He had spoken about how it worked and the opportunities it presented for learning and effective practice. As soon as he stopped, a hand shot up.

"Question?" Argyris asked.

"That's a nice theory," the student said. "But I don't think it will ever work."

"What would lead you to call it a nice theory, if you don't think it would ever work?" Argyris asked. The student looked puzzled. Argyris tried again.

"What is the purpose of a theory?" he asked.

"To explain things," she answered.

"OK. If this theory doesn't work, it doesn't explain anything, right?"

"Right."

"So what is nice about a theory that doesn't explain anything, if the purpose of a theory is to explain?"

The student began to answer, saying that it was nice because it was neat and tidy and internally consistent. All her criteria were ones Euclid and Ptolemy could have met with regard to their theories. For a few minutes she held onto her previous attraction to and approval of "neat and tidy" theories—for a few minutes, until something clicked. Suddenly her whole demeanor changed; she broke out in a smile and then a laugh. She laughed and laughed. As those in the class recognized what she had finally accepted, they laughed with her. It was an incredible moment in a room of 125 doctoral students as they experienced themselves stepping back, crossing the line to fourth-order thinking and double-loop learning, a thousand years after Ibn al-Haytham's friends had done the same. We can only wonder if his friends laughed too.

Rooting Ourselves in Concrete Data

The discipline of holding to the data is crucial to making accurate assessments and designing effective practices. All of the other techniques we share will help to some extent when incorporated into your practice. When used with attention to the data, however, the techniques we are talking about will transform your world the way they transformed a millennium. Asking for information, relinquishing "the obvious," even if it is comfortable, tidy, or appealing, opens incredible windows of opportunity. As you allow alternative realities and perceptions a place in the conversation, your world will expand, as it will for the people with whom you work.

What an irony, that a key to stepping into the outer reaches of fourth-order thinking is knowing when to stop and consult the concrete data. Constructing sound questions and theories on a fourth-order level begins by standing on terra firma. The better you become at locating yourself on the ladder of inference, the more likely you will be able to climb down when you need to. When we are rooted in the security of directly observable data, it becomes possible for us to tolerate the ambiguity that results from pushing back to ask the fourth-order questions. With the data as a stabilizing reference, the insecurity the answers often generate for us becomes tolerable.

This dynamic that enables us to remain flexible, resilient, and responsive while maintaining our own identity is the same dynamic we learn to cultivate in our faith life. With our security rooted in a trusting relationship to God, we are able to be responsive and flexible, rolling with the unexpected that comes our way. There are things we as human beings can know and for which we are responsible. There are things which belong only to God, for which we are not responsible. When we know that and know the difference, we are positioned to work and act effectively in the worldly arena which God has given us. Knowing that God is God, and we are not, allows us to remember our limits and our responsibilities, checking our context and our calling. Grounded in God's call and our earthly context, we find that the value of effective service emerges and the ineffective value of control can fade. Grounded in God and the earth, we can live with the ambiguity of life.

CHAPTER 5

Constructing Your Own Case

We have presented you with quite an array of skills and techniques to enhance your professional practice. And we have presented them while alerting you to the phenomenon of designed blindness. You have been reading about skillful religious leaders who have been caught by their own designed blindness, repeating errors even when they believed they should have known better. So it is reasonable for you to wonder how you are to learn, appropriate, and incorporate these skills into your practice if you too function within a framework of designed blindness. Good question!

The Use of Case Studies

The best way we know to uncover theories-in-use and break through the barrier of designed blindness is to take critical incidents and write them up as case studies for analysis. The writing alone creates some distance from your behavior and the event. That more objective position will enable you to perceive gaps and inconsistencies that you could not detect before. The case does not need to be about a crisis or traumatic event. Any time there is an interaction or event in which your behavior or the outcome puzzles you, there is an opportunity for learning through a case study. To make it worth the effort, and to produce insights from which you can build effectiveness skills, the case must be about a nontrivial matter about which you care.

Most people respond ambivalently to presenting cases. They are both attracted by the desire to learn and repelled by the exposure. They anticipate that presenting a case will be embarrassing, if not painful. Over time, as more people experience the transformation presentation engenders, the opportunity to present a case becomes a gift of high value. At the end of a year of presentations, some say, "I wish I had presented earlier, so that I could have used the year to practice and apply my learnings." Others say, "I wish I had presented later, when the group was more skilled, and I understood more about what was going on. I could have made even better use of the presentation." What we believe the ministers are pointing to, and what many of them have confirmed, is that they are aware not only of how far they have come, but of how much farther they still want to go. They learned a great deal but want to learn more. Their increased understanding and skill enable them to break through the designed blindness and develop an awareness of vulnerability and exposure.

One Sunday morning after worship, people were gathered for refreshments in the fellowship hall of Third Avenue Church. At one end of the hall two children about two years old were playing near the stage. The big stage curtain came down to within a foot of the floor. The two children had scooted behind the curtain. Those watching could see the children's arms and legs and movements. All that was hidden by the curtain was their heads. The children, on the other hand, were having a wonderful time hiding, believing their behavior was in secret. When those children develop the skill to understand that they were in fact visible all the time, they may have a feeling of vulnerability and exposure because they will now know that what they thought was hidden was apparent. But in actuality, their vulnerability and exposure will not have changed. People had been watching them all along. What will have changed is their awareness.

Practitioners who engage in this process recognize that some of their theories-in-use have been the source of their ineffective behaviors and understand that designed blindness is operating to keep them unaware. They become acutely aware of the need for an ongoing source of trustworthy feedback—feedback that will help them stay close to the directly observable data, and that will engage and challenge their reasoning processes. To be out in the professional world without these protections feels like driving a car without fastening the seatbelt. Certainly it has been done, and often without negative consequence, but when there is a collision, the seatbelt may be the only thing that keeps the driver in place while he or she recovers control of the vehicle. Aware of the pitfalls inherent in the ways they used to behave, these religious professionals ask what they can do to further the internalization of this new behavior, and how—in a self-sealing, Model I world—they can continue to learn.

Those questions are poignant for the people who have been a part of a supportive class of colleagues and are now faced with the dispersal of this trained and trusted community. These questions also challenge the reader, who has been part of the virtual community of learners encountered by reading this book but who needs to find a way to engage in this process and internalize the methods to become more effective in his or her practice. In the next chapter we will discuss recruiting and developing communities of accountability. You also need tools you can use alone.

It is possible to make great leaps of learning without ever presenting a case. You can recognize yourself in others' cases and feel your own cognitive dissonance in response to their presentation. But the drive to protect our own self-image makes learning difficult. Even if you believe the best way to learn is to present a case to a group and receive feedback, you may not always have access to a venue in which to work through this process. But there is something you can do.

It is helpful to write up your own cases for yourself. Often the *writing itself* is an effective intervention. Writing the case creates a vehicle through which you can retrieve much of what you once knew but of which you were unaware at the time, bringing it forward for your scrutiny. Writing allows you to get the distance you need to be able to discern incongruities and errors. Here is a description of how we recommend you write up your own case for reflection and learning. After that we offer some tools and techniques to help you engage in this learning and discerning process.

How to Choose a Case

What is most important, because it will offer the best return on your investment of time and energy, is to begin with a case that puzzles you in some way. It may be that you do not understand what happened, or why it happened, or how you might have handled the situation differently. It may be a case in which you felt particularly ineffective, or believed that you did something that you know made matters worse. It may be a case about which you have been ruminating without resolution.

It is important that this not be a trivial issue, but one about which you care. We are at our most blind and our most brittle when we experience ourselves as in danger or under stress. We turn to our most well-practiced responses and behaviors when matters of importance to us are on the line.

These well-learned responses often can be traced back to our childhood. They are automatic. As a result, at the very times when we most need to be open to hearing and learning, we are least likely to be able to do so. It is in such events that the most basic of our theories-in-use drive our behavior.

It is, therefore, in just such cases that we are more likely to be able to discern those most elemental theories that get us into trouble and to craft alternatives that would better serve us. For your maximum learning, choose a difficult situation in ministry that troubles or confounds you, and write up your case. Such a choice will offer the most sweeping and transportable changes.

A written case need not be long. In fact, too much verbiage is often a distracting nuisance. Keep it as focused as possible.

In writing the case, begin with a brief preamble introducing the situation and the characters. Basic factual information that would help a reader understand what is going on should be included. Any recognition you might have of presuppositions and assumptions you brought to the event could be identified. Then you move into recounting the dialogue.

It is important to recognize that there is more than one dialogue occurring at any given time. One is the external dialogue which everyone present can hear. It includes the nonverbal communications everyone can witness. The other dialogues are the internal dialogues going on in each of the participants' heads. Since this case is about you, constructed for your learning purposes, the dialogues in which we take an interest are both the external and public one and the private ones that take place simultaneously in your head. We often have more than one commentary and more than one evaluative process running at one time. Sometimes several voices in us are observing the same phenomenon but making different meanings of it. We may have a critical voice, which evaluates each participant's behavior, and a compassionate voice, which is caring or even protective. We may have voices that hurry us along, ones that hold us to our agenda, ones that ask questions, and ones that discern incongruities. Often a conference is going on in our heads, although we end up speaking with only one voice, and often that spoken voice says something quite different from what the dominant conversation in our heads has said.

In another kind of commentary, we observe and evaluate our behavior. You may find it useful to think of that commentary as the director's script. The director has a plan of how things should go and why. The director has theories about effectiveness. These are theories-in-use that set the goals and objectives and create the strategies intended to achieve them. The director may comment on our state of mind, our anxiety, our insecurity, our feelings of preparedness or vulnerability. That voice may speak in tones other than our own natural voice, calling up parents or teachers or others from whom we learned to evaluate and judge ourselves. All of the voices—the director's, the internal dialogue (of which we are relatively aware), and the audible external voice—are significant.

In writing up the event, create three columns. Each column should have a generous margin, allowing enough space for you to enter your analytical questions and commentary. On the right-hand side record the actual spoken dialogue, verbatim, to the extent that you can recall it. In the middle column, which I call the left-hand column,[1] write your thoughts, feelings, ideas, observations, and evaluations of what was happening while you were engaged in the interactions. On the left-hand side of the page (which I have come to call "left-of-the-left") write your "meta-commentary" as you watched yourself during the event. This left-of-the-left column reflects your director's script. It should record, to the extent that you can retrieve it, the ongoing assumptions, commentary, and assessments you make as the event unfolds. Your left-of-the-left column is likely to be fairly sparse when you first write up the case because so much of what it contains is outside your awareness. After working with the case, you may surface more of your assumptions and the scripts they generate.

In other words, what I want you to do is create a map of the multiple conversations (and the meanings you have attributed to them) in which you were engaged simultaneously. Each of these conversations, those inside your head and those you speak aloud, affect the other. They also affect the people with whom you are engaged (even though they are unaware of some of the conversations!). By visually spreading out these simultaneous responses side by side, you will have allowed yourself to take a step back and see relationships between the different internal voices and how you moderate and manage them. You will also be able to see the congruence or the disjuncture between what is going on in your mind and what is happening externally. It is often startling to realize the extent to which the people with whom you interact are being expected to react to information (commentary, beliefs, expectations, evaluations) to which they are not privy because you have not told them. So much of what you have experienced as part of the case has probably been private, undisclosed to other parties involved.

What the Case Write-Up Shows

Like a topographical map that reveals the levels of the land and the ways in which mountains and valleys connect or diverge, this map begins to develop in visual form the topography of your case. Recognizing how difficult it is for you to retrieve the reasoning processes that led you to the choices you made is a valuable learning on its own. You may discover leaps in your own thinking. Attributions that once seemed grounded in the events of the case you may now see were your private beliefs. Never tested, these perceptions may well be peculiar to you alone. Confronting the data before you, and recognizing that what you thought was obvious is in fact not supported by directly observable data, is the beginning of an exciting and fascinating detective operation. Now you uncover the reasoning that led you to the conclusions you drew and crafted the blindness that produced certainty about something that was inferred or attributed but never tested.

As you read these instructions, the case you want to puzzle over may already have come to mind. You may know just what has been troubling you or about which you have been ruminating for years. The idea of getting some clarity and closure can be energizing. But maybe the event took place so long ago that you can't be sure of remembering the conversations verbatim or reconstructing all the relevant facts surrounding the case. That is okay. Make them up if you have to. Don't worry about that. You see, this case is about *you*, and the learning you seek is about *you*, *your* thinking and *your* behavior. Your perceptions and the meanings you made of them matter far more than the events.

Remember, you cannot make up something that is outside your conceptual framework, something that is not you. So even if what you make up is a little different from what was actually said or what actually happened, what you are writing is still about you, who you are, what you think, and how you understand it. Remember, "No matter where you go, there you are," even in a case that relies only on your partial memory. It is still all yours, and you can still learn from it.

Analyzing Your Case

Now you have chosen a case that still troubles you. You have captured the context, recounting the setting, the players, and their relationships. You have probably struggled to retrieve the three columns of dialogue. The struggle to capture your case in writing was likely twofold. First, there was the simple difficulty of remembering what happened, in what order, and how you thought and felt about it. Second, there was the difficulty of revisiting an event that had been distressing the first time and probably remains so. You have worked hard as you re-engaged. Appreciate that. You have begun to learn. Simply entering into the process of taking what has been pondered inside and externalizing it, giving it a chronology and placing it within the matrix of relationships, has been an intervention. The analysis has begun.

Frame the Questions

The next step in the analysis of your case is to identify your questions and your learning goals. These admittedly may change as you go through the process, but it is helpful to have identified your initial questions and goals as you begin. Eventually, when you have done much of the work on your case, you may want to revisit the questions you framed. They may still have energy, capturing puzzles you are working on. Or insights generated in the analysis may reveal that the very way in which you framed the questions prevented you from seeing clearly and reflecting on your actual practice. This analysis is a dynamic process in which you pose questions, try to answer them, put together some pieces of your puzzle, and then reshape your questions.

What To Look For

Here you begin the analysis that opens the door and illuminates what had been hidden by designed blindness. You will go through each column in your case more than once. The first time you will identify attributions, evaluations, and assumptions. This is the beginning of a simple process which, when followed, will enable you to be increasingly effective in diagnosing your own case and bringing to consciousness the beliefs, attitudes, and assumptions of which you had been unaware.

Go through the text of each column of your written case. Focus on the language that is specifically yours (either spoken or unspoken, feelings or thoughts). Identify each statement of yours that is an inference, attribution, advocacy of some kind, or an evaluation.

- An inference or an attribution is anything about the other person which you believe to be true of him or her that was not part of the directly observable data. It may be an inference or attribution about meaning or feelings, about intent or expectation, about relationships or state of mind. An *inference* is made in response to data. You infer the meaning or feeling from what you observe, but it is high up the ladder of inference, and is not the data itself. *Attributions* are even farther from the data than are inferences. They may be based on generalized categories (for example, women are mechanically inept; men are logical), or may simply be qualities or behaviors we associate with that person, or what we believe to be that type of person.

- *An advocacy* is the act of putting forward your opinion, perception, point of view, or ideas. It need not be adversarial or in any way confrontational, although at times it may be. Advocacy is simply the act of identifying your position.

- *Evaluation* occurs when you determine the value or meaning of a happening. Evaluation may be positive or negative. It may be about a person or a situation (for example, "This meeting is going nowhere," or "He is never going to get it").

Having studied the dialogue portion of the case, turn your attention to the introduction you wrote (background, context, set-up), identifying inferences, attributions, advocacy, and evaluations there as well.

Note: Inference, attribution, advocacy, and evaluation are all important and valuable parts of communication and dialogue. Do not assume that their presence is in and of itself a problem. What we will be looking at is how those attributions, advocacies, and evaluations are formed and used, and in what ways the reasoning processes that produce them might be improved to minimize error and allow for correction.

For example, an attribution that someone is upset is likely to be a good hunch. Having formulated that hunch, it is necessary to seek directly observable data to confirm, refute, or refine that hunch into valid information.

Once you have gone through and identified these behaviors (we use the term behaviors to include thoughts and feelings, expressed or not, in addition to your external actions), go back to the beginning. At each identification of an inference, attribution, advocacy, or evaluation, ask yourself if the reasoning in your statement is illustrated and explicit or unillustrated and implicit. Notice also whether you asked any questions about these views. Did you test them either publicly or privately to confirm or discredit them? In what ways did you test them? Was your testing open and authentic? Did you check for directly observable data?

Dyer, for example, attributed agreement to her staff when they did not speak further about their preferences for salary reviews. Out of that attribution of agreement, she made a further attribution of consensus and acted on that "data." She did not test that attribution of consensus, either publicly or privately. She did not share her reasoning process, nor did she inquire. Consequently, neither her views nor her reasoning could be confirmed, challenged, or corrected.

Identifying Model I Social Virtues

Find the places in your cases' text in which Model I social virtues of supportive help, respect, integrity, or strength were the motivators of your behavior. Use the chart of the Model I Social Virtues in chapter 2, page 19 as your guide. Identify places where the Model I consequent governing values (such as unilaterally controlling the agenda) directed your actions. Consult chapter 2 to refresh your memory of these consequences.

Dyer's embrace of the Model I social virtue of integrity (stick to your values and principles; don't cave in) led her to back herself into a corner. She had attributed dishonesty, betrayal, and sneakiness to the staff for having privately told the personnel committee something different from their publicly agreed-upon policy. She attributed to herself integrity, honesty, trustworthiness and loyalty for having advocated with the personnel committee for the agreed-upon public policy. As a responsible advocate and representative of the staff, she believed that she had dutifully promoted the staff's position at the personal sacrifice of her own self-interest. Therefore she identified the presenting issue as one of principle. The principle Dyer upheld was standing by your word. She skillfully used her Model I strength (show capacity to hold your position in the face of other's advocacy) to defend her Model I integrity. She felt virtuous and trapped. The sad irony is that her staff felt virtuous and trapped as well.

Identify Consequences

So now through practice you have achieved distance on your case. You probably have enough distance to discern elements that had been invisible to you before. Go back through the entire case, beginning with the introductory material, and consider the consequences in each place thereafter where you have identified an advocacy without inquiry, or an attribution or evaluation without a public sharing and testing of your view, or where you shared (or advocated) a view without offering your reasoning behind it. What were the consequences of operating out of Model I social virtues? What were the consequences for you and for the others who were affected by your actions or inactions? What happened as a result of unilateral decisions you made? Were your decisions based on directly observable data, or on assessments made high up the ladder of inference? And how could the outcome have been different? What difference would an inquiry or a public sharing and testing of meanings have made at a particular juncture?

The consequence for Dyer of engaging in attributions that were not tested either publicly or privately, and for which she did not share her reasoning, was escalating error. She had made an error in her attribution, which led her to misrepresent her staff to the personnel committee. This action led to feelings of frustration and distrust of her reliability by the personnel committee, frustration and distrust by the staff that she would actually advocate on their behalf, and frustration and distrust by Dyer of her staff. It also led her to the further evaluation of betrayal, and of the staff as team-breakers and sneaks. All of these evaluations and attributions were in error and generated hostile working conditions, making mutual understanding and resolution much more difficult. Her intention of being virtuous, of being a team leader acting with integrity and strength, created more frustration and anger because she carried out these roles in a way that made detection of error impossible. It was not until the evaluations and attributions were coupled with publicly shared reasoning processes that Dyer and her staff were able to understand what went wrong and why each felt abandoned and betrayed.

Diagnosis/Invention/Production

Diagnosis. The next step in the process is to choose a point in your case where you believe an intervention could have made a difference, or where doing something different would have resulted in a better outcome. Referring to one of these intervention points, write out as clearly as you can what you think is problematic. Try to be aware of ways in which you might have made errors in your left and left-of-the-left-hand columns. (More often the errors occur there, before they are manifested as external behavior.) Some of these might be errors of untested attributions and evaluations, some might be advocacy without inquiry, or inquiry that is "fishing" rather than clearly and publicly advocating your position. Some of the errors might be in the ways in which Model I social virtues were driving your behavior. You may have been seeking to maintain unilateral control or to minimize negative feelings by telling people what they wanted to hear. What were the consequences of that behavior that you can now discern?

Invention. Consult the Model II Social Virtues Chart in chapter 2, page 27. Taking one specific segment which you have diagnosed, develop an alternative plan. Consider the following components as you craft your invention. Given the case situation and the new understandings you have realized, how would you change your thinking? Your strategy? Your goals? As you invent alternative behavior, reflect on your relationship to the other people in your case. Consider your expectations and intentions in relation to them. Would your expectations change? Your intentions? Does the message you now want to communicate differ? Why are these new goals and intentions important? Are they open to learning?

Production. Create a new script for this segment. Using your learning from the diagnosis and the development of your alternative, write a script in which you implement the plan you have just invented. Spell out just exactly what you would think, feel, hear, do, and say. Write out all three columns. Make sure that you illustrate your attributions or evaluations and that you do so using directly observable data. Couple your advocacy with inquiry, not only inquiring about the other person's perceptions, beliefs, and reasoning, *but inviting him or her to inquire into yours.* Create an interactive script, imagining how the others might respond, and crafting next steps to create a bilateral process open to correction and learning.

Then look at what happened. You may be surprised by your new outcome. It may or may not match what you had expected or intended.

After you have played out the new script, are there new questions for you to consider? Given the new outcome, do you still adhere to your original diagnosis and invention? Have you had new insights that suggest you could refine them? You might try rewriting the script again with the refinements and adjustments.

This kind of exercise need not be limited to segments of dialogue. Try using this method with your introductory background piece as well, if you have identified key diagnostic points there.

Revisit your original questions, puzzles, and goals for this case. Now that you have a deeper understanding of yourself, your professional practice, and the case, have you addressed the questions and goals you posed? In the case of those yet unanswered, what do you perceive as barriers? For those successfully addressed, what previous barriers have you overcome? What equipped you to make that progress?

Some of these questions or goals may no longer seem appropriate. Did they themselves reflect the errors on which the case was built? Might these discoveries help you craft better-formed goals for yourself and your learning?

I am asking you to pose many questions for yourself. To the extent that you take the time to reflect on them as learning devices, this action/reflection process will help you consolidate and fine-tune your learning.

I want this learning to equip you for the future. Your reconsidering the past is for the purpose of distilling elements that will be helpful for your ongoing ministry. Using this case, can you identify cues that signal the beginning of predictable behavioral sequences? You are looking for patterns that you repeat in other settings. Identifying the cue that starts the sequence will help you recognize that you are at a choice-point when such a situation presents itself again.

Recognizing that you use a well-learned behavior that is ineffective, use your invention to design an alternative behavior you might consider, should you find yourself faced with such a situation in the future.

Congratulations! You have just engaged in double-loop learning. It is "double-loop" because in addition to adjusting your strategy to achieve your goals, you have re-examined your goals. You have asked whether the outcomes you had set were the best ones for you. You examined them for congruence with your espoused beliefs, and were able to bring them into better alignment with your faith-based values. You were able to change your strategies and the goals they served to be more effective as a religious leader.

The model we took you through for double-loop learning, when mapped, looks like this:

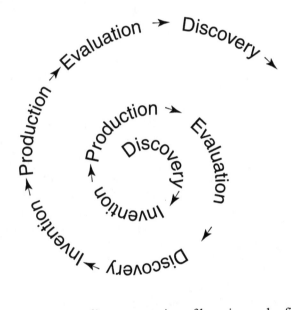

—thus creating an unending progression of learning and refinement.

Analyzing a Sample Case

Let us look at an actual case written up by the minister of a small church and practice this discipline of analysis. Using tools you have learned, we can identify some components of the case that led to the minister's ineffectiveness and frustration. In this particular situation, the case as presented did not include a "left-of-the-left-hand column." Nevertheless, it is a rich case. It demonstrates how much learning can be gleaned from a single page of dialogue.

CASE: THE SLIPPERY SLOPE

During fellowship following the Sunday morning service, the pastor (P) and the parish committee chair (L) were "visiting and idly chatting." The nominating committee chair came up and said, "She (L) just turned down becoming treasurer." The pastor isn't sure this nomination is a sound one, but puts that aside.

L1: I'm not good with finances and investments.

Why, that's not accurate!
You were treasurer of fund-raising and did a fine job. What is really going on?

P1: But you did the fund-raising treasury and did a good job of organizing it. Investments are different, I guess, but with your interest there are ways to learn. Maybe a different perspective would be good for us. Is there some other reason you are saying no?

I wonder if she will tell me. I suspect that it is because her partner is leaving the post of music director...and she did say at the parish committee that 12 years in a leadership position is enough for anyone. I wonder if she meant that for ministers too. She became the most animated at that meeting when the treasurer announced he was resigning, so I thought she was interested.

L2: I don't know how to work on investments. It is not an area I know.

Is she wanting affirmation? Is she just making conversation?

P2: I think the trustees need to have some vision, policies and direction. Investment knowledge is secondary.

L3: No. I don't know enough.

What does that mean? Do I dare ask? She has that "Don't bother me" look.

P3: I hear and respect your decision, but what are your thoughts on my ideas about needing an organizer, vision, policy person? Your history is long. Your input is valuable. You know what would work for the church and what is needed.

After all, she is still chair of the parish committee. Doesn't she want to think about the future needs of the church? I heard her say no, but can't she move from the personal to the professional?

L4: I just don't want to do it.

I already said that I heard you. Why won't you engage in discussing a different understanding of the role to help me and help the nominating committee?

Pastor's comment at the end of the case study: "I feel like I stepped into something that is very slippery and dark and under the surface. I want to learn how to surface the undiscussable."

First let us examine the overall pattern of this interaction. Bring to mind the social virtues and how they are reflected in the case. The principles inform-ing the social virtues govern the action, and we can see the predictable result.

Attending to the Social Virtues

Pastor begins (P1) with offering Model I helpful support, which means "offering approval and praise, minimiz[ing] disapproval and blame." What-ever concerns the pastor had about L's performance are not acknowledged.

When that support does not produce progress in the direction the pas-tor desires, unspoken challenges emerge in his left-hand column. These are not voiced—either for testing or to be acknowledged as potential concerns. This withholding of questions and concerns regarding L's reasoning (is this the result of her partner's job change, does she think ministers should leave after 12 years, is she needing affirmation, she had that "don't bother me" look) is the embodiment of the Model I social virtue of respect: "Do not challenge other people's reasoning processes. Their reasoning process are undiscussable."

The pastor continues making left-hand-column assumptions based on a Model I understanding of helpful support and respect. He wonders whether L wants affirmation (support), and feels reluctant to ask if that is so (re-spect). Caught in an interaction that appears to be going nowhere, or at least not where he had intended, the pastor flips his strategy while remain-ing within the framework of the Model I social virtues. Resorting now to Model I strength, which means "showing your capacity to hold your position in the face of another's advocacy," he presses his point (P2). In response to L's clarity about her position and what appears to be intransigence, the pastor responds with a rewording of essentially the same message, demon-strating both Model I strength and integrity (stick to your values and prin-ciples; don't cave in).

We begin to see how the consequence of the Model I social virtues is a series of governing variables that produce ineffectiveness. (The chart of these governing variables is in chapter 2, page 19.) The ground on which the pastor stands must shift as he attempts to put into action incom-patible and conflicting social virtues. The predictable unfolding of the con-sequences of the social virtues is the slippery slope which the pastor is feeling under his foot.

Applying the map of Model I behaviors as presented earlier, we can observe the predicted behaviors inevitably produced. The pastor is attempting to achieve the purpose as he has perceived it, which is to recruit L as the new treasurer. He is trying to maximize winning and minimize losing for himself, while also trying to minimize eliciting negative feelings from L. Although the pastor is feeling emotional (having been invested in the expectation that L would become the next treasurer), he opts for a strategy that holds to rationality and minimizes emotionality, thereby ensuring that the emotional issues in which he espouses interest will remain unsurfaced and unexamined. A self-sealing loop has been created, within which learning is compromised and effectiveness impaired.

Looking at the dialogue in the case with the tools developed for diagnosing a case, we can recognize a series of untested evaluations ("That's not accurate!") and untested attributions ("I suspect that it is because her partner is leaving" and "she became animated. . . . I thought she was interested") in his left-hand column. In addition, he identifies inquiries in his left-hand column which remain private and untested ("I wonder if she meant that for ministers too? . . . Is she wanting affirmation?"). These questions never see the light of day. His right-hand column, the actual dialogue of the case, with the exception of the last line of P1 ("Is there some other reason you are saying no?") is a consistent advocacy script. He makes repeated attempts, with slight changes in language or approach, to win the argument for his point of view and to get L to change her mind.

He says he respects her decision, but he does not inquire so that he might understand it. He has no information about her reasoning process. He has traveled way up the ladder of inferring her motivations. He does not test them. He then constructs arguments that are responsive to the concerns and interests he attributes to her. He does not ask if the concerns he is addressing are hers. He does not ask if he has correctly identified potential motivators for her. Then he gets angry and frustrated because, in his view, she is resistant.

He does not share his reasoning processes with her. Neither does he encourage her to ask him about them. She is left to make her own inferences and attributions about what is driving him. Within the context of a Model I interaction, it is unlikely that she would feel free to question the pastor's reasoning processes without an invitation to do so. As the chair of the parish committee, she would most likely, in public interactions such as this one, wish to be respectful of her pastor. In a Model I world, questioning the pastor's reasoning process would be disrespectful.

As you can see, they are caught in a self-sealing loop. Until inquiry becomes a part of the interaction, significant information is lacking, and the means for accessing it are barred.

Each of these dimensions of analysis would probably not be apparent to you, had this been your case. It was, after all, the puzzling nature of it that led you to write up your case in the first place. It is likely, though, that one of these dimensions of Model I would become visible to you as you reconstructed it and studied the written case.

The simplest analyzing process—identifying advocacies, inquiries, attributions, inferences, and evaluations—led this pastor to notice when looking at the actual dialogue that he was running a straight advocacy script. This helped him realize that L began to withdraw and shut down in reaction to his unrelenting pressure. He was trying to win her to his point of view. With that one insight, he was able to consider other available options that would allow for more authentic dialogue. As he sought to construct possible alternative conversations, he became more aware of the difference between his private internal dialogue and his public statements. He began moving his unspoken questions into his proposed spoken dialogue.

The new conversation he invented was much more open. He was surprised to discover that even in this imaginary conversation, his attempts to maintain control had caused him to lose control of the unfolding of events. That level of frustration led him to wonder what other barriers were preventing him from engaging in an authentic bilateral conversation. It was here that he surfaced what would have been in his left-of-the-left-hand column, had he been able to recognize it earlier. Driving much of this interaction was a belief that when any member of the church turns down a position, it is a negative commentary about him. He experiences it as a vote of no confidence and a public expression of his inadequacy as a pastor. He had been unaware that he held that belief. His left-of-the-left-hand column, the ultimate director of his behavior, was strategizing with an intense desperation that did not reasonably match the issue at hand. He had believed that his very self was being threatened. By understanding the primitive theory-in-use that was driving him, he was able to challenge himself to relinquish a dysfunctional belief.

The pastor tried again to rewrite his script. In his newly invented dialogue he became a partner with L in discovery. The control issues became irrelevant.

Any place where you can interrupt your case has the potential of breaking the self-sealing loop that has trapped you. Systems are such that if you change one part, the rest of the system is changed too. Begin with small insights and simple interventions. Pick one thing you wish to do differently. Write up the case as you now might imagine it. Even with the small change, you will have added options and identified choice points at which the alternatives can be considered. You will be able to take that small change and implement it each time you recognize a choice-point. The change will happen a little at a time. The benefits, however, will be cumulative. Increased effectiveness will become a part of your professional practice.

CHAPTER 6

A Community of Learning

During the war in Vietnam, the American forces sought to prevent the Vietnamese from crossing rivers. To that end, they sent bomber planes to destroy the bridges. Much to their dismay, Vietnamese by the thousands continued crossing the rivers. When the bridges were thoroughly bombed out, the traffic continued, baffling the Americans. Later, when the Vietnamese were asked how it was that they were able to move so many people across the rivers, they replied, "We built the bridges six inches under the water."[1]

Stuck in Assumptions

It is easy to get stuck in assumptions that prevent us from perceiving alternatives in both meaning and interpretation. Once locked into a particular assumption (e.g., all constructed bridges are visible and above water), we believe that assumption to be true, that it is obvious, and it is data. When other data come in that don't fit, we are puzzled. It is difficult to recognize that the puzzling results we receive actually refute our inferences and assumptions. Because we have embraced the inferences and assumptions as data, in our minds they are already established as fact. We do not apply corrective feedback that suggests an error in our thinking, because those "obvious assumptions" are considered data in our minds.

It takes someone from outside the situation to recognize the gap and raise the illuminating questions. That is why consultants can be helpful. This tendency to misperceive the difference between hard data and assumptions leads us to recommend that those of us who practice ministry create a consulting community of sorts.

To accomplish your best thinking, your best problem-solving, your most creative responses, you will need someone to ask, "What if there are bridges you cannot see?" and "How would you know it?" Those questions are unsettling, but they open the mind and often the heart to that which is present but yet unseen.

The Bridges of Vietnam

This story is a gem because in its simplicity it offers a powerful teaching parable. A true story, it becomes a metaphor about how the world, and therefore churches and their leaders, function. Sometimes congregations dismantle institutional structures that they believe are creating or maintaining unhelpful or outmoded behaviors. In dismay, they scratch their heads as the old ways of communicating and doing business continue, despite changes in formal structure. What the leadership has done is dismantle the formal and visible infrastructure.

That strategy is not unlike the Americans removing the visible bridges in Vietnam. All the while, the people continue to use the informal networks and systems they have learned so well. These are unwritten, unofficial, well-known systems, the strong and resilient infrastructures that operate, much like the Vietnamese bridges, under the surface. Because they are tacit, not public, and not acknowledged, these structures are also often undiscussable. No wonder it is so hard to sort out what is happening!

Clergy are just as vulnerable to this behavior as are the congregation and its lay leadership. In some ways, the underwater bridges represent our theories-in-use, the ones on which we actually walk and which drive our ministries. We build big fancy bridges of espoused theories. They stand up tall and proud for all to see. Sometimes we use them. When the sun is bright, and the wind is soft, and the day quite balmy, we use those bridges of espoused theory. When we are in no particular hurry, or don't really care when or how we arrive, we will use the fancy public bridge.

As the going gets rough, we relocate ourselves, and it is another story. When the storms gather, when we feel our safety is at stake and our position precarious, when we want to be certain that we have control, we don't walk out on the bridges that are publicly constructed and visible. We do something different. We turn to the protected, hidden bridges known since childhood. Walking in the ways once learned so well, we feel comforted and secure.

We feel secure because this way of behaving is well-practiced and tacit. It is like the knowledge a gymnast has when performing on the balance beam. The knowledge is no longer conscious but embodied, integrated into our whole being. To replace this with conscious, thought-out behavior is very difficult, especially under pressure.

As a result of this tacit nature of our response, we may seldom notice that we have abandoned the public bridge. Or we may think that the people with whom we work will not notice. We are usually not aware that the gap exists. Others challenge us, perceiving the incongruity. We proudly point to the public bridges of our espoused theories of ministry, church, and faithfulness, and offer reassurance. But all the while we are walking along on another bridge, one they cannot see, cannot challenge, six inches under the water. We think we are safe. And we wonder why people get exasperated and disturbed.

A Community of Inquiry

Who will tell us that they know the bridge we are on is not the bridge they can see? Who will tell us that the system by which we live is not the one we profess but rather the one that remains suspended, hidden from view, six inches under water? And who, when we are in the position of the Americans soldiers, trying to accomplish a mission that is failing for indiscernible reasons, will raise the question, "Are all bridges always above water?" For it was the inability of those on the American team to ask that question that doomed them to defeat.

We need a community of inquiry. Such a community *cherishes its critics*, those inside and those beyond, because it understands that the prophetic voice and the word of God are often spoken by those we do not really want to hear.

Ronald C. Arnett, professor of interpersonal communication at Marquette University, calls this kind of community an ethical community. Drawing from theologians Martin Buber and Dietrich Bonhoeffer, Arnett suggests that:

> The essence of a lasting ethical community requires a conscious commitment to labeling and examining the shortcomings of the community. Shielding the community from scrutiny or criticism is

not of long-term benefit to the organization. A community can only strive to be ethical by listening closely to its critics.[2]

With Arnett we believe that the kind of community we seek to develop is ethical in profound dimensions. The ethics of Model II are based on the respect and honor of each person. It is an ethic that recognizes the spark of light each one carries to illuminate our common darkness. The Model II ethic resolves to protect and defend the light of life and wisdom against the winds of convention and fear. The ethics of Model II demand a hermeneutic of consultation and consent.

People are not subjects of our actions, nor objects of our contemplation. As Martin Buber advocated, the other person in Model II is cherished as a "Thou," someone with whom we are in relationship, and not merely a player on our stage. The Model II learning community is ethically based in that it understands that learning is life-loving and affirming. Such a community also understands that denial and blindness lead to stagnation, alienation, and spiritual death. Circumstances may present us with the choice of life or death. This choice was put before our ancestors in Deuteronomy 30:19: "I have set before you life and death, blessings and curses. Choose life, so that you and your descendants might live." Model II teaches us how to recognize and choose life.

Learning in Community

To the extent that you can be part of an authentic and open community of inquiry, you will be more likely to discover what you need to know. To the extent that members of your community are committed to your learning and theirs, they are more likely to raise difficult questions and observations publicly. To the degree that the participants are able to embrace and embody Model II values, errors will be discovered and corrections invented. Such practices help create faithful and ethical communities. For such a community to emerge and be sustained, there must be those within its ranks who understand and affirm this charge and this call. Still, the task is difficult.

Because you are trying to change *yourself*, and because you have become so skillful at designing your own blindness, you will need others, those whom you trust, to be truth tellers for you. You need people who can give you the feedback you need to hear. They will tell you, even if you are the emperor, when you are wearing no clothes.

People can do the difficult and loving work of giving and receiving honest feedback in authentic community. Authentic community is forged and deepened as its members build relationships based on the kind of respect, support, and integrity Model II engenders. In such an open and honest learning environment, community thrives. It releases the power of the creative spirit that calls and empowers you to do your holy work.

Such a community is built a few steps at a time. You begin with small learning groups where people build trust, learn skills, and deepen their commitment to be faithful to the faith, to God, and to this community to which they have been called. Changing tacit behavior patterns takes time and practice. The "coaching" of a community helps all of its members improve bit by bit.

The Jewish and Christian traditions have consistently taught that faithfulness requires community. Part of the community's responsibility is to be a place of learning. Wisdom is mediated through the community of the faithful. The community accomplishes this mediation in many ways. It interprets its tradition, renews its covenant, and is accountable to the future, the past, and the present, for its behavior and the consequences. Wisdom is dynamic and engaged, constantly evolving because it is about learning.

Community Practice

The faith traditions that we serve have long understood that community building practices are suitably undertaken in groups of various sizes. Common worship usually is expressed in larger groups. The Jewish tradition requires a minimum of ten (a minyan), whereas the Christian tradition requires only three (where two or three are gathered in his name), yet for most of our communities the practice of common worship occurs in groups far exceeding those numbers.

Other practices are better done in small groups. Study is one. Study may take place in the context of an intense one-to-one student-teacher relationship, or in small groups or classes. Bible study most often occurs in relatively small groups, where there are enough opinions to stimulate thinking, but enough time for everyone to speak who wishes. Usually these smaller study groups operate within the context of the larger faith community. That community is enriched and its practice deepened by the leaven provided by the small group of learners.

Action Science and Small Groups

The context in which the possibilities for learning action science are maximized is the small group. Within the small group, trust can build. People covenant together as learners. They share their experiences and their puzzles. Together they begin to uncover the gaps and inconsistencies in their behavior. They develop skills and attitudes that enable them to tell what they have seen and heard each other do. They thus hold up mirrors for one another, reflecting back observed behaviors. The participants break through the barriers of designed blindness which they had constructed.

The members of the small learning group benefit directly. Auspiciously, the interdependent nature of systems results in an ever-expanding impact. Larger groups from which these smaller learning groups were drawn are in time affected. A new culture in which learning is a driving value gets introduced into the larger system by the members of the small groups. The organization is strengthened by its effective practitioners, who create new options by embodying learning behaviors wherever they function.

Constituting Learning Groups

Small learning groups can be drawn from within the ranks of a particular faith community, from a group of congregations that choose to work together, or from the interfaith community. Although for reasons of theological reflection some may prefer to be with people who share their religious tradition, we have found that it is not necessary to do so.

The learning groups could consist of clergy who seek to improve their professional practice. Lay leaders who wish to improve their practice of leadership and interaction can covenant to be a group. The groups could be a mixture of clergy and laity, or each could choose to have a distinct group. It doesn't matter.

What does matter is that those who join:

1. Are interested in learning.
2. Are willing to experience the discomfort of confrontation with reality.
3. Are willing to risk being transformed.

As they are transformed, so will the world as they know it be transformed. In joining the groups, those who participate must understand that they are giving their consent to those life-changing transformations.

Getting Started

The size of established groups may vary from setting to setting. Yours could have as few as two or three members, or as many as 15. Having a designated facilitator helps the process during the initial phase. It is also important to be explicit about the length of commitment the group is asking of its members. Groups do best if they work together for a year. Skills and trust build over that span of time to forge effective feedback loops and learning. It is possible to make some progress over a six-month period. But the shorter the time frame, the more difficult it will be to integrate skills and learnings so that they are useful and retrievable in real time, when you need them. However long you contract to meet as a group, your design should include respectful closure at the end, and the possibility of some members choosing to continue. Two hours a week provides enough time to engage each other deeply. This is intense work. Keeping the time to two hours allows people to maintain a high degree of attention and focus.

The Covenant

Developing a covenant within which to work builds group trust and facilitates the growth of effective communication and healthy relationships. The group is to be clear and honest with one another about expectations of membership. Then it is easier for participants to engage in the challenges and vulnerabilities that nourish learning. Some of these expectations may be simple and straightforward, such as regular attendance and punctuality. Some may be more difficult to grasp or honor, such as respectful engagement, suspension of judgment, and the right of each person to set his or her own boundaries and to be responsible for his or her own learning.

It is helpful to begin with a tentative covenant, which is revisited after the concepts of Model I and II social virtues are presented and engaged. Often such words as "caring" and "respect" remain part of the covenant, but the group develops a new understanding of what that behavior requires of the participants. Other dimensions of the covenant may be changed as the group works together and people begin to understand the journey on which they have embarked.

Introducing Model II Skills

The facilitator needs to have some familiarity with action science. This book is a good beginning. The group will function best if everyone has read this book and begins the work with some exposure to the goals and concepts of Model II. In the absence of that common reading, the first weeks of the group should include some basic teaching of action science concepts.

Even for those groups in which the members have read the book, it will be important to give people time to engage in discussions that raise their questions, concerns, and puzzles about this process and approach. They will also be helped by describing the outcomes they desire for themselves. All of this processing, while it may seem time-consuming, lays the groundwork for the development of a community rooted in the values and practices of Model II.

For the work to go forward, the group should work on incorporating Model II values in its common life. That suggests that the governing values of maximizing information, sharing the development of the agenda, and taking bilateral responsibility for each other's well-being and success ought to be part of the group's culture from its inception, to the degree that leaders and members are able to do so.

It is possible to begin your group with the simple telling and sharing of personal experiences and stories. That opening helps members get to know one another. However, if the group is serious about intentional learning, it will soon begin using written cases. They provide the best material and the most compelling learning devices.

The people in the examples we have cited all used opportunities to present their troubling situations in the form of simple written cases—often just a page or two of dialogue, with accompanying thoughts and feelings and some contextual material. They used the model of writing a case which we presented in the previous chapter as a guide. Some were more successful than others in filling out all of the columns. All cases provided rich opportunities for learning by the presenter and the learning group.

Many groups adopt the practice of script-reading the dialogue before engaging in discussion of the case. This approach enables everyone to get an experience of the case, and allows the presenter to step back and observe his or her own behavior. It is usually most helpful to the presenter when the other participants take all of the parts so that the presenter can watch and listen. Should you choose this method, have someone read the left-hand column voice, and if there is a left-of-the-left-hand column, choose a voice for that as well. Allowing the players to report how it felt to play their roles is often illuminating to the presenter and opens up possible directions for the group to explore.

It is often helpful to appoint a case manager or facilitator. This person keeps the conversation on track, and ensures that everyone who wants to speak has the chance. The case manager relieves the presenter of being the gatekeeper of the group so that he or she can focus on the issues being raised.

The written case offers a basis from which the group can work. Once the work is started, it is easy to realize that each person's case is everyone's case. Model I is a strategy and way of being in the world at which we are *all* expert. The ways in which that model trips us up and exposes us to error are universal.

Using a Tape Recorder

The sessions were also tape-recorded. This practice enabled the presenter to listen to the tape a few days after presenting. With reduced stress and some distance on the event, more of the feedback could be appropriated and additional new learnings could be absorbed by the presenter while listening to the tape. It is important to listen fairly soon, when the presentation is still fresh and clear in your mind. Take notes while you listen. Capture your glimpses of what had been hidden from you. Write down your learning and share it with the group at its next session. That sharing will help you integrate the learning and will become feedback to your colleagues on what was effective and helpful in their interventions.

The recording is a learning tool. During the group's discussion of your case you are intent on listening to feedback from your peers while you are responding to it. There is not time to become self-aware. Listen to the tape by yourself. (Maintaining the group's confidentiality is important—even if the case is about you.) As you listen, the "previous you" who presented is "over there" in the recorder. You the listener can become aware of your other self: How does he (or she) sound? What is the tone, the volume, the pace? Is it changing? What was going on in the presenter's mind as the interaction took place? What can you learn about yourself from this perspective?

Listening to the tape, you can become your own coach. From what you hear, what alternatives can you conceive? What do you think you could say to the presenter that would be helpful? How would you advise him or her?

How Religious Professionals Use Action Science

Variety is the spice of life. We have shared a model for intentional learning which we know is effective. It is not the only one. Our colleagues in the field have found many ways in which to incorporate the kinds of feedback and Model II learning they need into their ministries. Creativity abounds. Here are a few ways religious professionals who are learning Model II have engaged its practice in their ministries.

In a Large Congregation

Rabbi Levy belonged to one of the learning groups that we described. It was his presentation in written case form of the puzzle with the sisterhood that enabled him to grasp the ways in which he was setting himself up for frustration and failure. He was so excited by what he had learned that he brought it back to his staff members. They were impressed.

As he continued in his learning group, he would periodically recognize new incongruities in his behavior. He would share what he had discovered at staff meetings. The staff members became envious. They too wanted to learn how to be more effective. They too wanted to be able to see in themselves what others perceived about them which they could not perceive themselves. They too wanted a group that would be authentically supportive and helpful. They wanted the kind of support the rabbi was getting to be part of their life together as a staff.

Levy and his staff members contracted to engage in the study of action science together, focusing on their work at the temple. In addition to regular staff meetings, they scheduled working sessions when Levy would teach the staff and they would learn together. Eventually, as they became more comfortable with the concepts and more capable of giving effective feedback, the learning group dissolved and the Model II behaviors they learned became a part of their staff culture.

The religious educator, the cantor, the school administrator, and the office administrator all changed the way they understood help, support, respect, integrity, and strength. They created a staff culture that reinforced Model II values. They ran their staff according to Model II governing values. The temple became a workplace in which people thrived and grew not only in skills but also in spirit. The laypeople noticed and asked for a group of their own. In time the culture of the temple began to shift. It was becoming a learning congregation.

In a Small Congregation

The Rev. Hal Johns served a small church in a suburban town. As he participated in a learning group with colleagues, his behavior began to change. He asked different kinds of questions at board meetings as he incorporated his learning into his behavior. The board conversations became more open. Frank Reynolds, a middle manager in a large technical firm, sat on the board and noticed the change. Reynolds had learned some new skills in his company's continuing-education program. His interest piqued by the changes at board meetings, he tried engaging in the same kinds of inquiry he saw his pastor doing. He liked the results.

Reynolds also noticed that often the pastor did not engage in that process of inquiry. He observed Johns using his power and influence to win approval of his position. Those times felt less satisfying to Reynolds. Often he left those meetings feeling frustrated or angry. When Reynolds became board chair, he took the pastor out to lunch.

"Pastor," he said, "I have observed the ways in which your behavior has changed since you joined that learning group. Sometimes your interventions really make a difference and help us to ask the right questions and understand what is going on. I appreciate that, and have been trying to learn from you."

His pastor was pleased and flattered. Reynolds went on. "When you use those skills, it is very good for the board. But you do not always use them. Sometimes you come on very strong. Sometimes it is difficult for people to disagree with you. Sometimes you are so focused on what you think should happen that you don't hear what others are contributing." Johns was sobered by this feedback and highly impressed with the new board chair.

Reynolds had a proposal. He thought it would meet his needs, and possibly the pastor's needs as well. "What would you say to making an agreement to meet with me the week following every board meeting in addition to our usual planning meeting? At that follow-up meeting we would give each other feedback about how effective we thought we were, evaluate the meeting and what we'd set as an agenda."

Learning from These Settings

Despite the differences in the settings, Levy and Johns both found that there were people with whom they worked who were excited by learning, and who could perceive the increase in effectiveness resulting from their work with action science learning groups.

In both cases the initiative and agenda for learning was bilateral and jointly owned. The people involved embarked on a process already formed by Model II governing values. The likelihood of success was therefore high, as was the possibility of discovering error and making the necessary corrections. In both settings, the energy of the professional ministry and the lay ministry was renewed.

In a Midsize Congregation

The Rev. Adam Cornwall had engaged in a clergy learning group. At his congregation's governing board meetings, whenever he heard himself speaking from high up the ladder of inference, he would stop. Realizing that he was making statements as though they were facts, when they were based only on his assumptions, attributions, or inferences, he would say, "I just made that up." He was disarmingly confessional. And he smiled. From there, he would try to retrieve the necessary data by asking others for confirmation or disconfirmation of what he had inferred or attributed.

This behavior had a noticeable effect on board members. If they found themselves discussing matters based on hearsay or inference, and for which they did not have supporting data, people would take responsibility for obtaining the missing information. Alternatively, if it was not possible or convenient to get the data, the board at least had become aware that it was making decisions based on conjecture. Without ever discussing his learning group or Model II, Cornwall began to notice that other people on the board would sometimes stop in mid-sentence, look at the others, smile, and say, "I just made that up, didn't I?" They had learned to check.

Communities of Accountability

Ministry should be practiced in a community of care and accountability. That is ancient wisdom. How that care and accountability are lived out is what we are opening for examination and enhancement. We believe that Model II behavior brings us closer to the congruent and authentic living of our faith as individuals in community. There are many ways to get there. We have shared the ones we have discovered to be effective.

You will need to practice using these tools to develop your skill. Just as when you practiced preaching or counseling, or comforting the bereaved, starting with awkward and tentative efforts, you will begin this effort with some unease. You are at the beginning base of the learning curve.

When you were learning basic skills for ministry, you probably benefited from feedback offered by supervisors, teachers, and peers. In field education you may have learned to receive feedback from parishioners as well. In your current situation, such feedback is essential. As we have seen, often that feedback itself becomes part of the your community's growth as a learning environment. Eventually reliable feedback will become built into your practice and, over time, become part of the culture of your institution. Feedback and receptivity to learning from that feedback will become the bridges under the water on which you and your community walk with confidence, day in and day out. This new behavior will itself become tacit, embodied. But you will know that you built it and can adjust it. You and your community will grow in creativity and wisdom.

An institution that learns how to learn will always be relevant, always be vibrant and always be hospitable to the movement of the spirit. Such a religious institution will cultivate and nurture people of God who are not frozen, not brittle, not stuck, but constantly growing in faith.

In a learning congregation people will recognize opportunities to be faithful. They will craft new ways to be God's people. The construction of bridges of community and communication will be ongoing. What kinds of new bridges you design will be limited only by your imagination. But we can make a prediction. The bridges you build will be public, effective, and invitingly beautiful.

CHAPTER 7

From Community Spirit to a Spiritual Community

Ministry is relational work. Clergy are called into relationship with God and with the other to whom we minister. Relationships require communication. We have examined the ways in which our thinking shapes our communication, and the ways in which our communication affects the effectiveness of our practice. The context of our practice is community, whether we are working one-on-one or in groups. We hope that people may experience belonging to a congregation with a common purpose and shared goals.

We engender community spirit when people experience a sense of individual agency and of their significance within the group. Both of these outcomes are valuable and to be encouraged. They help people become complete human beings. Theologian Paul Tillich spoke of the importance of these outcomes when he spoke about "the courage to be as a part" and "the courage to be as oneself."[1] Both of these kinds of individual courage contribute to the healthy and effective communities we want. But as clergy, we have another outcome that commands our attention.

We as religious professionals are concerned with more than building community spirit. Schools and corporations, philanthropic organizations, and service groups can all exhibit community spirit. They are not, however, explicitly spiritual communities. The task we face as religious leaders is to grow communities of faith. We share *educational* tasks with schools, the need for *fiscal responsibility* to our stakeholders with corporations, the development and sustenance of *caretaking* institutions with philanthropies, and direct *service* provision with service groups.

We are, however, distinctly different from each of those good organizations. The activities we share with them are not our primary mission. They are strategies—activities in which we engage to help us fulfill our primary mission of being a faithful people of God, a spiritual community.

The spiritual community undergirds and empowers the activities we share with other groups.

The Nature of Spiritual Community

Martin Buber affirms the centrality of community in Jewish spirituality and religious practice. He finds in the Hasidic tradition beautiful and effective descriptions of that spirituality.

> The Hasidic movement . . . teaches that the true meaning of love of one's neighbor is not that it is a command from God which we are to fulfill, but that through it and in it we meet God. . . . It is not just written, "Love thy neighbor as thyself," as though the sentence ended there, but it goes on. "Love thy neighbor as thyself, I am the Lord" (Leviticus 19:18). The grammatical construction of the original text shows quite clearly that the meaning is: You shall deal lovingly with your neighbor, that is, with everyone you meet along life's road, and you shall deal with him as with one equal to yourself. The second part, however adds, "I am the Lord." . . . the Hasidic interpretation, "You think I am far away from you, but in your love for your neighbor you will find Me; not in his love for you, but in yours for him." He who loves brings God and the world together.[2]

Buber finds God in the loving of the lover.

Jesus taught a similar understanding of how authentic religious practice provides a direct path to the salvific experience of God and God's grace. God is met in the authentic and compassionate encounter with the other. He finds God in the person of the one who is being loved, and explains this truth to his disciples in the Gospel of Matthew:

> Then the king will say to those at his right hand, "Come you that are blessed by my Father, inherit the kingdom prepared for you from the foundation of the world; for I was hungry and you gave me food, I was thirsty and you gave me something to drink, I was a stranger and you welcomed me, I was naked and you gave me clothing, I was sick and you took care of me, I was in prison and

you visited me." Then the righteous will answer him, "Lord, when was it that we saw you hungry and gave you food, or thirsty and gave you something to drink? And when was it that we saw you a stranger and welcomed you, or naked and gave you clothing? And when was it that we saw you sick or in prison and visited you?" And the king will answer them, "Truly I tell you, just as you did it to one of the least of these who are members of my family, you did it to me" (Matt. 25:34-40).

These examples from Buber and Matthew, coming out of the Jewish and Christian traditions respectively, both understand that it is in relationship that we evoke God's presence and render it accessible to the individual. It happens in community. That message sounds familiar and almost comfortable.

The Challenge of Loving the "Other"

There is a twist to the message though, revealed in the explications by Jesus and the Hasidim. The kind of community in which that happens is not what we expect. We are not invited to find God in the presence of those whose thoughts we already know, whose worldviews we understand, whose experiences confirm our own. We are invited instead to find God in the encounter with those who are distinctly different from us.

These different ones are those whose thoughts, feelings, expectations, and ideas are difficult to understand. Often they are so different that we find it difficult to accept the reality of the difference. Despite inevitable inaccuracy we attribute thoughts, feelings, and ideas to them. We find it easier to make attributions about these unknown others, keeping ourselves safely at a distance, thus avoiding the risk of actual encounter. We are not where they are, and we do not know what they know.

That is not to say that you who are reading this book have never shared any of the experiences or situations to which Jesus refers. You may have been a prisoner or a stranger, hungry or homeless, sick or lonely or naked. You may have known these circumstances personally and intimately. But in the specific situation Jesus poses, the responder is not at the moment in the same situation as the one in immediate need.

The prisoner and the visitor are having a different experience. The hungry and the provider of food do not share the same circumstance.

The one who is at home inhabits a different context from the one who is a stranger, and encounters the world from a more knowledgeable and probably more secure position. Jesus' challenge is profound, if we allow ourselves to grasp it.

Jesus is telling us that when we make contact with the one who is different, the one whose world is not like ours, we begin to allow God into our lives. When we let in the one whose assumptions surprise us, whose judgments conflict with ours, whose worldview disquiets us, and when we stop pretending that the differences aren't real, we have crossed the threshold into religious practice. It is in the practice of that kind of encounter that we begin weaving the strands of authentic spiritual community. It is just that authentic encounter that action science enables us to have.

Action Science as Spiritual Practice

Although it was not designed to be so, we find that action science, at its heart, is a spiritual practice. The discipline of action science enables us to have the skills and the courage to know the other and to allow the other to know us. Therefore, it helps develop a lived and faithful relationship with the divine. Because action science teaches us that the essential venue in which to engage the practice of faith is in community, it is congruent with our religious teachings and is also a vehicle for fulfillment of those teachings.

Action science takes us even more deeply into spiritual discipline than we might have anticipated. With the use of action science we begin to realize how distinctively "other" we are from each other. Certainly the one who is imprisoned knows a world different from the world of the one who moves in freedom, and the one who is hungry has a different experience of life than one whose stomach and larder are full.

But when we have made the insights of action science our own, we realize that each of us knows life differently. We are separate and unique individuals. Each of us lives in a different "world." Before, without thinking, we projected our own thoughts, experiences, and beliefs on those with whom we shared cultures, contexts, and opportunities. But now we have been awakened.

If we engage others, we are truly open to who it is that stands before us. We want to learn of that person's profound otherness without attributing thoughts, feelings, meanings, and intent with no basis in fact. Thereby, we begin again to know the holy. The irony is that only when we allow ourselves to make room for the other's *different* perceptions, gifts, and contributions, do we begin to encounter the *common* threads in our humanity. These are the threads that weave into us the image of God, and weave us into the beloved community.

Reality: Relocating the Center

In the spiritual community we cease being the center of our universe. We recognize that our maps of the world originated from our *interaction* with the world. They are our interpretations of reality, but not reality itself. There is a broader, thicker, richer reality which is accessible only through shared exploration.

The religious community commits itself to helping us discern a reality that is larger than ourselves and beyond our individual grasp. Our communities of faith, through space and over time, expand our horizons insofar as we seriously engage in that discernment process with them.

Not only do our covenanted communities introduce us to a larger universe; they hold us accountable to a transcendent reality. Honest, intentional, and effective discernment becomes essential as we seek to fulfill our spiritual responsibilities of establishing a right relationship with God and with each other. To the degree that our congregations become places where the people learn and practice disciplines that serve those goals, they become communities of reconciliation as well.

Action science, as a discipline, produces clarity where there was blindness, discernment where there was projection, engagement where there had been defensive self-sealing. It therefore becomes a spiritual practice that moves us toward reconciliation and experiencing the life of beloved community.

We understand that we can only "see in a mirror dimly . . . know only in part" (1 Cor. 13:12). Full encounter and understanding of the divine reality is yet to come, and we do not expect to realize in its entirety the vision we hold. Nevertheless, the task of the spiritual community is to look deeply into that dim mirror. We may not be able to see all there is to be seen, but we are responsible for seeing all that has been revealed to us. We are charged with knowing what is knowable.

In spiritual communities God is at the center, animating, sustaining, and connecting us. *Together* we seek to know and understand that in which we live and move and have our being. Despite our vast wealth of knowledge, there is mystery at the center, and things we do not comprehend. Spiritual communities need to be learning communities. When grounded in humility and a deep appreciation of all there is, we still have to learn that we are positioned to reach out with open heart and mind to one another and to the God who moves between. Action science, as a discipline for learning, becomes a spiritual practice.

A Theology of Humanity

Elie Wiesel, writer, Holocaust survivor, collector of Hasidic tales, and professor of humanities at Boston University, once said, "God made man because he loved stories."[3] Here is a contemporary story. It serves the purpose of a theological midrash, albeit in a lighter-than-usual vein. It may just be that the reason why the Bible is so short on humor is that God had great confidence that we would fill it in.

> One day there was a gathering of scientists. They spoke about all they had learned and what they had unlocked about the secrets of life. They could now clone life, and create it in a test tube. They had unlocked most of the secrets of DNA, or at least understood its principles sufficient to finish the task. So some of them went to God and said, "We thank you for all you have been and done for humankind, but we do not need you now. We can create life ourselves. We know how to reproduce it. We understand our biology. You can go now."
>
> God thought a moment about this and said, "I understand. But before we sever this relationship, could we have one test?"
>
> "Sure," said the scientists.
>
> "Let us each take a handful of earth, and create life."
>
> "Okay," said the scientists, and they selected their team.
>
> When they were ready they returned, and at the appointed time readied themselves to reach down and grab their handful of earth from which to begin.
>
> "Oh no," said God. "You have to get your own dirt."[4]

Our understanding of humanity is informed by our perceptions of human possibility, humility, and finitude. That understanding shapes our theology. We have come into a universe not of our creation. We have hope and vision that go beyond the present, but we work with what we get. We are humbled by our limits, encouraged by our genius, and ever held accountable to what is highest and holiest, the Creator God who is love.

The world contains within it human potential for growth, learning, and reconciliation. Yet it is also gripped by structures of human relationship that impede these possibilities. They wound and isolate people from one another and from the creative and generative forces of life.

We have created chasms among ourselves and between us and God. The societies into which we were born were structured in that way. We didn't start it. But we continue to create such wounding structures and teach our children to do the same. In doing so we have unknowingly designed social structures that perpetuate these chasms of isolation. We are left separated and ineffective. Model I is a map that describes how those structures function.

Model I and Human Sin

Sin is a human act in which right relationships are broken or distorted. Sinful acts are those that rupture our relationship with God or render it unsustainable. Sinful acts are those that are destructive of human relationship. They devalue people and dishonor or disregard the precious individuality of each person. When we locate ourselves inappropriately in relation to others or to God, elevate our importance, and presume our own centrality or infallibility, we sin. The Model I map of the world describes structures that distort interpersonal relations, put unnecessary stress on relationships, and treat people as objects rather than subjects, To the extent that this map becomes the framework for our thinking and the basis for our actions, it teaches, perpetuates, and sustains sin.

We once asked Chris Argyris if Model I was original sin. "I don't know anything about its being original," he said. "I just know that it is." Now, Model I is not necessarily sinful. At times it is useful, efficient, and effective. Most often those situations are simple, nonstressful, or routine. Model I is sometimes the right tool. When there are no glitches, and nothing significant is on the line, it can work just fine. But if there are errors, the situation changes. It is difficult to retrieve errors using Model I. It is difficult to ask double-loop questions or attain higher-order learning using only Model I. Its usefulness is limited. When used universally in response to every circumstance, it becomes dangerous. For most of us, it is the only tool we have.

The characteristic of Model I functioning that resembles original sin is its inevitability. Inevitably we will break faith, behave differently from what we intend, rupture relationships, and remain blind to having done so. We will sin. The sins that we address in this book are driven by Model I.[5] With the Apostle Paul we wonder how this can be happening to us.

> I do not understand my own actions. For I do not do what I want, but I do the very thing I hate. Now if I do what I do not want, I agree that the law is good. But in fact it is no longer I that do it, but sin that dwells within me. . . . For I do not do the good I want, but the evil I do not want is what I do. Now if I do what I do not want, it is no longer I that do it, but sin that dwells within me. So I find it to be a law that when I want to do what is good, evil lies close at hand. For I delight in the law of God in my inmost self, but I see in my members another law at war with the law of my mind, making me captive to the law of sin [Rom. 7:15-17, 19-23a].

Paul calls it sin within him. He finds in Jesus the saving power to face the cognitive dissonance, admit his errors, and learn what God has to teach him. Paul was not the first to notice that despite his wishes to live in God's ways, he was unable consistently to do so. In the book of Ecclesiastes we are reminded: "Surely there is no one on earth so righteous as to do good without ever sinning" (Eccles. 7:21).

In Judaism there is no concept of original sin. There is an understanding of human beings as having both the good impulse and the evil impulse. The goal of human living in Judaism is to use the Torah, Scripture, to leverage the good impulse. We can see in Ecclesiastes that it is a challenge that lasts a lifetime. It is never fully resolved. We are always engaged.

The story of the people Israel is the tale of a people who mean to do one thing and do another. They bind themselves in covenant with God to be a faithful, just, and righteous people, and are shocked time and again as the prophets call them to account, confronting them with the gap between their intentions and their actions. They, like us, are surprised and disturbed when the incongruity between their actions and intentions is identified.

Shout out , do not hold back!
Lift up your voice like a trumpet!
Announce to my people their rebellion,
     to the house of Jacob their sins.
Yet day after day they seek me and delight to know my ways,
as if they were a nation that practiced righteousness
     and did not forsake the ordinance of their God;
they ask me of righteous judgments,
     they delight to draw near to God.
"Why do we fast, but you do not see?"
     "Why humble yourselves but you do not notice?"
Look, you serve your own interest on your fast day,
     and oppress all your workers.
Look, you fast only to quarrel and to fight
     and to strike with a wicked fist....
Is such the fast that I choose,
     a day to humble oneself?...
Is not this the fast that I choose:
     to loose the bonds of injustice,
     to undo the thongs of the yoke,
to let the oppressed go free,
     and to break every yoke?
Is it not to share your bread with the hungry,
     and bring the homeless poor into your house;
when you see the naked, to cover them,
     and not to hide yourself from your own kin.
Then your light shall break forth like the dawn [Isa. 58:1-5a, 6-8a].

God wants them to do better. God wants us to do better. And we are reassured and sustained by knowing that God will love and companion us through the difficult process of recognition, repentance, and transformation, just as God has in the past. God forgives us; there is the chance to try again. Learning is possible. But always first there is the need for us to recognize that we have fallen short. We must, on some level, understand and acknowledge that we have been convicted in our error.

We did not do what we meant to do. We did not hear as we meant to hear, speak as we meant to speak, love as we meant to love. Yet often we are unaware that we have missed our mark and fallen short. That is what action science means by "designed blindness." Somewhere, somehow, in small groups or large, in the privacy of our prayer life, or the public place of a congregational setting, we need to be confronted by our shortcoming and then confess to the gap, that it might be healed.

This work, like all faith work, requires the exercise of discernment. Sometimes Model I is acceptable and can serve the good. Sometimes it can't. Sometimes Model I undercuts the values on which your faith is built. There are times when only Model II will enable you to act in ways that support your primary values. The goal of action science is to provide options—the chance to choose, and choose well.

A very traditional theology undergirds this work. It is the theology of transformation, reconciliation, and redemption, which permeates the biblical traditions. We find the spiritual wisdom of that theology incorporated in the liturgies of Yom Kippur and Holy Communion. Both Yom Kippur and the service of Holy Communion lead the worshipper through the process of confessing, turning, and healing. Always these are processes that include learning.

An Old Map Visited

The Pilgrim's Progress is a classic work by John Bunyan, originally published in 1678. Through that work, Bunyan, out of the Protestant tradition, attempted to describe the change process through which a religious pilgrim in search of redemption and reconciliation must go. He used the metaphor of travel to describe the morphology of the redemptive process.

Bunyan leads the reader through the phases of the journey one should expect to take as a seeker of God and salvation. He describes places, events, obstacles and changes the pilgrim is apt to experience. The journey is a useful metaphor. When we go through transformation, we experience our environment so differently that it is as though we were in a new location. We feel like travelers. We appreciate the signs and maps we are given to help us become oriented to new territory. The sacred histories we pass down within our various traditions, telling the tales of our transformed forefathers and foremothers, provide some of those maps. We value the reassurance offered us that we have not lost the way. Others have traveled this route before.

Action science posits a morphology of change congruent with the one presented by John Bunyan. *The Pilgrim's Progress* is a good case study. I share some snippets of it to assure you that you have not lost the way, and that others have successfully taken this route before.

The story opens with our sorrowful hero, Christian, encountering evidence that he bears burdens he is incompetent to remove. This is important because action science is a discipline designed to solve problems that cannot be solved without a shift in basic values, policies, and practices.[6]

> Behold I saw a man clothed with rags standing in a certain place, with his face from his own house, a book in his hand and a great burden on his back. I looked, and saw him open the book and read therein; and as he read he wept and trembled, and not being able longer to contain he brake out with a lamentable cry, saying "What shall I do?"
>
> The man ran to tell his family of his dilemma saying, "Oh my dear wife, and you the children of my bowels, I your dear friend am in myself undone, by reason of a burden that lieth hard upon me; moreover I am for certain informed that this our city will be burned with fire from heaven, in which fearful otherthrow both myself with thee, my wife and you my sweet babes shall miserably come to ruin; except which I see not some way of escape can be found whereby we may be delivered.[7]

Christian considers himself to be in a high-risk, high-stress situation from which he can see no avoidance or escape. Trapped, as he perceives it, Christian describes his experience:

> I saw a man named Evangelist coming toward him who asked, "wherefore dost thou cry?"
>
> Sir, I perceive by the book in my hand that I am condemned to die and after that to come to judgment; and I find I am not willing to do the first nor able to do the second.[8]

In this case, Christian's theory-in-use is this: When confronted with a threatening possibility, make predictions of doom and act as if they are inevitable. From the book he also infers generalizations which he believes apply to him, and which he then considers to be data. The interventionist in this case, the Evangelist, begins the process of making Christian aware of the inconsistencies embedded in his statement by using directly observable data drawn from Christian's own conversation.

Christian replies with much the same fearful response as at first. Evangelist then inquires into Christian's motivation for change. "If this be thy condition, why standest thou still?" And Christian answers quite simply, "Because I know not whither to go."[9]

It is fascinating that Bunyan's Evangelist over 300 years ago practiced some of the significant behaviors Argyris has identified with Model II. Argyris says: "Action scientists hold normative views about alternative ways of living . . . hence action scientists not only describe the world as it is and as it might be, but they . . . also specify how to get from here to there."[10]

At that point in the story the Evangelist gives Christian a parchment telling him to "Fly from the wrath to come," and when Christian asks "Where?" the Evangelist gives him direction, assuring him that he will be told along the way what to do.[11]

Christian and his friend Pliable head off and, being heedless, end up falling into a miry bog, the slough of Despond. Because of the burdens on their backs, they begin to sink. Pliable gets discouraged and, dragging himself out, sets off for home leaving Christian to struggle in the slough alone.

Action science predicts that people once caught in the trap that Model I thinking has set will become emotional, beginning with bewilderment, then vulnerability, anger, and fear. Bunyan's hero does it all.

> Then a man came to him whose name was Help. And asked him what he did there?
>
> "Sir," said Christian, "I was bid to go this way by a man called Evangelist who directed me also to yonder gate that I might escape the wrath to come. And as I was going thither I fell in here."
>
> Help: "But why did you not look for these steps?"
>
> To which Christian replied, "Fear followed me so hard that I fled the next way and fell in."[12]

One of the premises of action science, as it seeks to enable people to shift from Model I perceptions to Model II possibilities is that we first need to be convinced of our own error and the lapses in our effectiveness. We need to be helped to discover our own incompetence, to recognize that the solutions we invent do not adequately resolve our problems.

These short excerpts from *The Pilgrim's Progress* illustrate the task that faces religious leaders who would open up the world of Model II alternatives for themselves and others. We must first do it for ourselves before we can effectively do it for our parishioners. The quotations illustrate our journey as frustrated and discouraged professionals. But "Evangelist" also shows us how to be teacher, preacher, and coach for others.

The process is difficult, and never completed. As Methodism's founder, John Wesley, put it, we are "going on to perfection," but never get there. There will always be times when we construct our reality with Model I maps. There will be times when we are under stress that we slip back into the very behaviors that got us into trouble in the first place, defensive routines that we know so well.

In that element, action science is also congruent with the general expectations of the religious life. We are always growing in faith. We will always have lapses, moments of doubt, moments when we are frightened and cling once again to the magical God of our childhood. Neither action science nor religion expects us to get it perfect. They are both grounded in the deepest realities of the human experience—spiritual, psychological, social, intellectual. Action science reflects a theology of humanity that is profoundly loving, forgiving, and hopeful—and also stark in its identification of our flaws and vulnerabilities.

With Argyris, I believe that we are acculturated into a Model I world. It is a way of being in the world that we learned early and therefore exquisitely. As flawlessly as most of us have learned to drink from a cup or eat soup with a spoon, we have learned the Model I social virtues and the techniques of unawareness.

Can We Be Led Out of the Wilderness?

What was once learned can be unlearned. What knowledge we have accrued by accumulation can still be added to. Model II is a challenge, but it is not out of reach. As with moments of grace, when we are operating within it, we feel the joy, the blessing, and the presence of God in our lives.

This God who informs Model II and shapes its ethic is a relational God. We share the God of theologian Martin Buber, for whom God dwells in the moments of authentic connection between people. This is the God whose presence is ever on the "narrow ridge" that holds fast to the importance of maintaining relationship to others without relinquishing accountability to our principles.

We refuse to allow another person to become an object and insist upon the full and respectful encounter with the other as "thou" (or in today's language, "you"). This practice is what characterizes our behavior as profoundly religious and redemptive in nature. Others are not means to our ends. They are not resources available for manipulation to serve our purposes. Each must be engaged as a distinct individual. Each is to bring his or her own wants, needs, hurts, and dreams to the table. This work presumes a theology in which the image of the holy is reflected in every relationship. That image is to be held sacred and is not to be transgressed.

The image of the holy dwells within each of us, even as it is in the other, and in the relationship in between. We are relational beings even within ourselves. We can fully encounter and approach the God who indwells only when we also understand the parts of ourselves that serve other masters. When we engage in designed blindness, we prevent ourselves from knowing who we actually are. We forget whom or what we have chosen to serve. We dim the light of the Imago Dei in us. We hide it. Designed blindness takes our light and puts it under a bushel basket. It prevents us from knowing what really is within us. It conceals from us who we yet could learn to be. In short, it estranges us from ourselves. Designed blindness allows us to transgress the holy that dwells within.

We Can Be Changed

Many of you know the song:

> Amazing grace! How sweet the sound,
>   that saved a wretch like me!
> I once was lost but now am found,
>   was blind but now I see.
>
> 'Twas grace that taught my heart to fear,
>   and grace my fears relieved. . . .
>
> Through many dangers, toils, and snares,
>   I have already come;
> 'tis grace that brought me safe thus far,
>   and grace will lead me home.

John Newton, who penned those words more than 200 years ago, was a slave trader bringing captured Africans to the American shores to be sold into slavery. Slave trading was legal. It was a thriving business. It was sanctioned by most of the church. It was wrong.

John Newton was a religious man, a Christian. One day the scales fell from his eyes. He let go of the unending work of creating and sustaining his designed blindness, and allowed himself to stand in the pain of cognitive dissonance, convicted of his sin. When he dropped his denial and defensiveness, then the horror of his sin, his deep engagement with evil, and his estrangement from God became apparent to him. What he had been doing was in conflict with the essence of his own religious sentiment and its moral imperative. He had once been blind, but now he could see. And he stood before God and the truth with fear and trembling.

Newton celebrated that experience of fear as grace. It was his hour of truth, of discovery. That precious moment opened up the possibility of another way. He now had a new chance to seek right relationship and reconciliation with God and other people. Newton, unassumingly humble and contrite, is a model of learning to grow in grace. Rather than hiding from the confrontation with his behavior and its consequences, he embraced it, naming it grace. "'Twas grace that taught my heart to fear."

Grace didn't stop with fear. He also understood the healing, saying: "And grace my fears relieved." Grace allowed John Newton the possibility of change. Grace allowed him to turn once again, and walk back into the arms of God. Grace allowed him to know that there is a difference between the essence of a person and his or her actions. If Newton could repent and learn a new behavior, God and grace would lead him home.

That Grace May Abound

Action science is about hating the sin and loving the sinner. Action science hates the sin, exposing the often destructive and ineffective nature of our behavior, and its incompatibility with our most highly cherished values. It loves the sinner by teaching us the ways in which we can close the gaps, minimize the hypocrisy and reconcile the damaged relationships which our behaviors have engendered. It loves the sinner with a deep trust in our desire and longing to do the good. Action science, from that position of affirmation and care, encourages us, the sinners, to acknowledge our errors.

It seeks our willingness to accept appropriate guilt, and take corrective action. It is not about shame. Many times we frantically keep drawing the shades in our mind's eye, trying to stave off the conviction of error. We mistakenly believe that if we are found to have done something wrong, we are wrong, rather than understanding that we have done something wrong. We make errors. We are not ourselves errors.

Shame-based thinking prevents us from knowing what we need to know to be responsible and faithful. It leads us to think we are wrong. If so, there is little we can do. We cannot change ourselves. But we can change what we do. When we are able to face our guilt (the wrong we have done), we can let go of shame (the sense of ourselves as being wrong).

Grace (God's acceptance) can save us in our wretchedness because through grace we experience God's love. Through grace we are taken out of shame-based, destructive understandings and carried into the landscape of love. Authentic love, human and divine, loves the one who really is before us, and not the person we wish he or she were. Love allows for error and sin, because it also allows for growth. Grace, forgiveness, and love are present, accessible, and available. They can find us and lead us home. Before we can follow, before we can be led home, we must acknowledge that we are lost, that at times we are afraid, that we have strayed. Action science as a spiritual practice permits us boldly to acknowledge our sin, that grace might abound.

CHAPTER 8

Putting It All Together

One day through the primeval wood
a calf walked home as good calves should;
but made a trail all bent askew,
a crooked trail as all calves do.

Since then three hundred years have fled,
and I infer the calf is dead.
But still he left behind his trail
and thereby hangs my moral tale.

The trail was taken up next day
by a lone dog that passed that way;
and then a wise bell-wether sheep;
pursued the trail o'er vale and steep
and drew the flock behind him too,
as good bell-wethers always do.

And from that day, o'er hill and glade,
through those old woods a path was made,
And many men wound in and out,
and dodged and turned and bent about,
and uttered words of righteous wrath
Because 'twas such a crooked path;

But still they followed—do not laugh—
the first migrations of that calf,
and through this winding wood-way stalked

because he wobbled when he walked.
The forest path became a lane
that bent and turned and turned again;
this crooked lane became a road,
where many a poor horse with his load
toiled on beneath the burning sun,
and traveled some three miles in one.

And thus a century and a half
they trod the footsteps of that calf.
The years passed on in swiftness fleet,
the road became a village street;
and this, before men were aware
a city's crowded thoroughfare.

And soon the central street was this
of a renowned metropolis;
and men two centuries and a half
trod in the footsteps of that calf.

Each day a hundred thousand rout
followed this zigzag calf about.
and o'en his crooked journey went
the traffic of a continent.
A hundred thousand men were led
by one calf near three centuries dead.
They followed still his crooked way,
and lost one hundred years a day;
for such reverence is lent
to well-established precedent.

A moral lesson this might teach
were I ordained and called to preach;
for men are prone to go it blind
along the calf-path of the mind,
and work away from sun to sun
to do what other men have done.

They follow in the beaten track
and out and in, and forth and back,
and still their devious course pursue
to keep the path that others do.

They keep the path a sacred groove,
along which they're compelled to move;
and how the wise old gods must laugh
who saw that first primeval calf.

Ah, many things this tale might teach—
But I am not ordained to preach.

—Sam Walter Foss, 1895

The poet who wrote this charming spoof is almost as obscure as the primeval calf about which he writes. His message, by contrast, is plain and accessible. Foss captures with wit the irony of our Model I lives and the conviction under which we stand. His ability to step back and reflect the absurdity contained within our self-sealed errors gives the experience of our own incompetence a humorous context. Comic relief is welcome. We can join with Foss, laughing at ourselves, as we recognize that what is laughably ineffective is also part of our common human experience. We share our dismay and frustration with the generations, if not as far back as the primeval calf, as least as far back as anyone can remember.

With Foss, we also share a hope and a conviction. It is not necessary to be entrapped in the well-worn rut of what has been. We do not have to:

go it blind
along the calf-path of the mind,
and work away from sun to sun
to do what other men have done.

We can see that what we have been talking about in this book is not new. If it could be known to Foss more than 100 years ago, it could have been known to us by now. What is new, and what we have offered you, is a way to recognize the well-worn groove of ineffectiveness when you have entered it, and some ways for you to get out. As your skill level increases, you will even be able to recognize the groove before you step into it, and begin instead to craft a better path that will get you where you want to go effectively and efficiently. While Foss steps back and laughs at our blindness, we are equipped to do more than smile ruefully at the human condition. We can interrupt the design, and begin to see our options.

We opened our exploration of effectiveness in professional practice with three cases, those of Rabbi Levy, Sister Gellerd, and Pastor Dyer. Each of these people was a highly successful and intelligent religious professional who was puzzled. They were frustrated with the inexplicable (to them) conundrums they encountered in their practice of ministry. I believe they are not alone. In fact, I believe that their experiences are replicated across this continent and beyond. You probably have had such experiences yourself.

I predict that under stressful circumstance, in difficult situations dealing with nontrivial issues, each of us will create situations that are not what we intended. We will behave in ways that produce unintended consequences, will make errors we cannot identify, and will remain blind to how we have done so. I predict this because in the 15 years of my work with religious professionals, combined with Chris Argyris's 30 years of work with other professionals, we have consistently witnessed the masterful practice of the skills that produce such ineffective behavior. We have all learned exquisitely well how to design our behavior so that we remain blind to the ways in which we contribute to the problems we seek to solve. I call this complicated and high-level skill "designed blindness." The mastery of this extraordinary skill and its incorporation into our professional behavior have resulted in the strange but real phenomenon of skilled incompetence. No wonder you and others are often puzzled.

This book was written with the recognition that you are therefore already quite skillful at what you do. You have mastered much. Now that you have already learned and mastered the set of skills that produce ineffectiveness, you can learn others. With practice, applying the tools you have learned here, you can design opportunities for learning where once you had designed blindness. While conundrums may still occur, and puzzles will continue to appear, you now know how to go about solving these riddles. Always, it begins with you.

Back to Our Colleagues

We learned that truth with our colleagues Levy, Gellerd, and Dyer. Levy began with the puzzle of what was wrong with the women in the sisterhood. He wondered why such seemingly nice women would behave so unfairly as to ask for his help, refuse it, and then blame him for being uncaring and unhelpful. He presented a case about them. At least, that was how he had framed it. He was shocked and dismayed to discover that the case was about him, not the women in the sisterhood. He then understood that the ways in which he had approached the situation and the responses he had given the women had been the stimulus for the negative spiral of disintegrating relationships.

Levy was also liberated. Because he could identify errors in his behavior and in his understanding of what was happening, he could also correct them. Whereas before his bafflement had left him feeling helpless and like a wrongly accused victim, now he felt the power to act. The responsibility he carried was no longer a burden because he had acquired what he needed to make his load manageable.

In Dyer's case, puzzlement was exceeded only by frustration and rage. She had been a collaborative leader, had consulted others, and had been willing to champion her staff members and their preferences. They had betrayed her, declining to use the collaborative opportunities provided. They had broken faith with her and with each other.

She brought her case to the table wanting to figure out how to deal with and manage this untrustworthy staff. In light of their behavior, she wondered if they were too childish and irresponsible to participate in collaboration and collective decision-making. Maybe they were simply too self-centered. She asked herself, "Was all the attractive theory about collaborative leadership a hoax? Was it a bad idea, or were the folks on my staff just not competent enough to handle it?"

Dyer had two outside references on which she focused her puzzle. One was the theory of collaborative leadership. The other was the staff. Was the theory wrong? If it was, that would explain what caused the problem. Was the staff incapable of responsible collaboration? If it was, that would explain the cause of the problem. Dyer, like Levy, came to talk about "them" and discovered that it was she who had brought the seeds of the failure to the case and cultivated them into flower and fruit. Her harvest was no longer a puzzle. She was able to recognize that she was reaping what she had sown. The embarrassment she felt when she first understood that it was she who had undermined the collaborative process gave way to relief and exhilaration. The new understanding meant that she was not surrounded by self-centered and unworthy staff, incapable of collaborating responsibly. It meant that she did not have to relinquish her dreams of developing a collaborative leadership style. And, since she had been instrumental in the breakdown of trust, she now recognized that she had the power to begin the rebuilding.

Gellerd brought her case to the table looking for support and ideas for how to deal with colleagues who were selfish and uncaring. She had lost respect for them as they appeared to put institutional and financial concerns above the schoolchildren's welfare, which she understood to be to the teachers' highest responsibility. She felt discounted by them, silenced and powerless. When she had finished working with the group on her case, she came to realize that the case was more about her than it was about her colleagues.

When Gellerd finally realized that her friends and colleagues had not ignored her or her student's issues, she was astonished. She had never given them the chance to respond because she had never told them what she thought or wanted. As she recognized the ways in which she had set them up to disappoint her, and realized that she had been the cause of her own silence, she became excited. In addition to recognizing that she was working in a friendlier and more supportive environment than she had thought was the case, she was learning how to be a more effective advocate for her students. She could recognize how she had been part of the problem when the teaching staff tried to develop a realistic strategy for getting the children's needs met. Now she could be part of the solution, and a powerful one at that, because she would no longer silence herself, or give her power away.

Model II: A New Map of the World

What the Model II principles did for our colleagues' case interventions was to give them a new map of their world. The new map was one of greater flexibility, creativity, and opportunity. In the new map they were neither trapped, powerless, nor mired in the "slough of despond." The new maps of their worlds were peopled with colleagues, parishioners, and co-workers who were more well-meaning, less hurtful, and better-intentioned than in the previous maps. All of this happened because Levy, Dyer, and Gellerd changed. When they exchanged the Model I map they had been employing for a Model II map, their perceptions were altered, their internal dialogue shifted, the ideas they came up with changed. All of this resulted in significantly different behaviors, increased effectiveness and enhanced morale. Instead of sliding down a spiral of frustration and multiplying errors, they began riding on a rising tide of energy and excitement.

The most important challenge before you is the challenge to redraw your map of the world. If you operate with the Model I social virtues, engaging in interactions directed toward goals you have unilaterally determined, trying to control the people with whom you work, perceiving the others as competitors and manipulating events so that you can win, the strategies we suggest will not bring you closer to your goal. Behavior driven by and serving Model I values will be self-sealing and antilearning. Technique will not help. The meanings you make of the world you encounter, the possibilities of which you conceive, the position in a system in which you locate yourself and the nature of the relationships you maintain, are all part of your map of the world. It has been Model I, but it can be transformed. Creating a Model II environment begins with creating the map. Equipped with the new orientations provided by the Model II map, your internal dialogue, your feelings, and your responses are transformed, and the new world you mapped becomes visible, right before your eyes.

The tools we have given you are designed for use in the new map. It is as though we had just taught you how to use a screwdriver. You may have actually obtained one and put it in your toolbox, ready for the opportunity to apply it. However, if you still buy only nails when you go to the hardware store, you will not be able to employ your new screwdriver successfully and productively. Creating the new map, and using it to navigate is like buying the screwdriver and the screws. You can begin building in earnest.

Basic Toolbox for the Effective Practitioner

What follows is a summary of some of the key skills presented in this book. By collecting them here, I hope that you will be able to use this final chapter as a ready reference and reminder. Remember, the steep part of the learning curve is slow-going. The summaries here may keep you focused and inspired when you feel clumsy and awkward while trying something new.

Social Virtues as Building Blocks

The social virtues are the foundational building blocks for all the other behavior. They shape the goals, objectives, and strategies that drive you. You may use our tools, and you may invent new ones. If they are governed by these social virtues and their governing values, they will produce behavioral practices that are open to learning, and will increase your effectiveness.

MODEL II SOCIAL VIRTUES

1. Helpfully support people.
    This means:
    - Help individuals to become aware of their reasoning processes.
    - Help them become aware of gaps and inconsistencies.

2. Respect people.
    This means:
    - Human being are capable of and interested in learning.

3. Be strong.
    This means:
    - Behavior reflects a high capacity for advocacy coupled with a high capacity for inquiry and vulnerability without feeling threatened.

4. Maintain integrity.
    This means:
    - Advocate and act on your point of view in such a way as to encourage confrontation and inquiry into it.

Directly Observable Data

To the extent that you can recognize and refer to directly observable data in your explorations, inventions, decisions, and evaluations, you will ask more useful questions, produce better solutions, draw more realistic conclusions, and make more reliable and accurate evaluations.

Remember: Directly observable data is that information which you hear, see, smell, touch, or experience directly. It is without meaning content.

Facial expressions are directly observable data, if you can capture the expression (for example, a furrowed brow) rather than the meaning you would ordinarily ascribe to it (puzzled).

Words spoken are data (for example, "I don't know what you are talking about!"). The meaning you would ordinarily make (You are an idiot!) is not there, and is not part of the directly observable data.

Smells noticed (like a burning sulfur smell) are often hard to separate as data from meaning (someone struck a match).

The data are concrete realities. The meanings we ascribe to them have the possibility of error. To the extent that we can know whether we have is data or whether what we have is inferred or attributed meaning, we will be better equipped to discover errors and make corrections as necessary.

The Ladder of Inference

The ladder of inference represents the way in which we move from directly observable data to more complex and abstract levels of meaning and interpretation. We do it all the time. It is necessary that we do so. However, each time we climb a rung of the ladder, the possibility of error exists. Although it may be too cumbersome to check every time we ascend a rung of the ladder, the payoff for checking increases as we go higher.

Most of our decisions and strategies are determined on the level of "meanings imposed by the actor in the situation," if we are the one acting in that setting. Often we are making decisions and acting on information that was given to us by someone about others. (A committee chair consults with the minister about handling a situation in the committee). At such a time, we are working on the highest rung of this ladder ("meanings imposed by the consultant in the situation"), because as pastors in that setting, we are functioning as consultants. We will be well served if we can retain the humility that is ours when we recognize just how little we really do know about a situation for which we have no directly observable data.

LADDER OF INFERENCE

4. Meanings imposed by the "consultant" in the situation
3. Meanings imposed by the actors in a situation.
2. Cultural meanings.
1. Directly observable data.
Earth.

Identifying Cues

We run up the ladder of inference very quickly. We have had a lot of practice. Because it is second nature, we do it automatically, usually without thinking, just as we do not need to think much about how we shower if we are able-bodied. It is something we simply do. To interrupt that process so that we might stop and consult data, or check for error, we need some kind of markers or flags that will help us find our way back down the ladder to earth. We each have our own idiosyncratic ways of stimulating the run up the ladder of our mind. Something cues us to do that. Identifying cues in our own processes allows us to interrupt our mental scampering and to become aware of where we are in relation to the data.

We experience our internal cues in the form of thoughts, words that come to mind, or feelings that trigger an automatic set of responses. These first responses are often self-sealed and unhelpful. Identifying the cues allows us to make a choice to let the familiar routine play itself out or to decide, "No, I'm not going there this time."

We may miss the internal cue and find that we can still catch ourselves by identifying external behavior cues. We may notice that we have started drumming our fingers on the table, we may hear ourselves say something in our parent's tone of voice or phrasing, or we may recognize that we have crossed our arms across our chest. Again, the behavior will be particular to you. To the extent that you can recognize that what you are doing is the beginning of a behavioral routine, you will have created a choice point to continue, or to do something different.

Twin Tools: Advocacy and Inquiry

The tools of advocacy and inquiry are integrally linked like conjoined twins. Each is relatively dysfunctional when used alone, and powerfully effective when used together. Used separately, they discourage learning. When they are employed together, learning becomes possible for everyone.

When we advocate for our position or point of view without inquiring about the other's position, we create a situation in which the other is likely to be defensive. Our behavior suggests that the other point of view is unimportant and would not add value to the conversation or decision-making process. In response the other person is likely to feel the need to protect and defend it. We may not ever get to learn what it was, since we did not ask him or her to put it on the table. Our continued advocacy may lead the other to believe that sharing an opinion would put him or her in the line of attack, rather than open a dialogue of mutual exploration. Alternatively, when confronted with our untempered advocacy script, the other may respond with parallel behavior, running an alternate advocacy script and championing that position or idea. We now have escalating advocacy without inquiry. We may end up with a winner, but with very little wisdom.

Inquiry is a way of finding out what others think. Asking outright is the clearest, most direct, and most effective tool for inquiry. When we inquire, the other person experiences himself or herself as being acknowledged and valued. Through our inquiry and the other's response, both become participants in a relationship and a process. It is generally a good thing. However, inquiry used alone can also become anti-learning.

If the inquiry stands alone and does not include our advocacy and ownership of our own position, we have not created a field for dialogue and authentic exchange of ideas. We have set up a situation that is inherently unjust, in which we have asked the other to be vulnerable and to take the risk of putting his or her ideas out in the marketplace, while refusing to take that risk ourselves. The learning that would come from the mutual exchange and exploration of ideas, their strengths and limits, has been prevented by the one-sided interaction. Our ideas may be safer that way, less vulnerable to scrutiny, criticism, and change, but they are also probably less useful than they could have been had they been subject to a conversation of correction and refinement.

Sometimes inquiry is insincere, and merely serves as a ruse for leading people to agree with our own position. In that case it is not truly inquiry, but advocacy masquerading as inquiry. Asking leading questions that serve our own agenda is sometimes called "easing in." Easing in as a strategy is a popular Model I technique. When we initiate an easing-in script, we usually think of ourselves as being gentle, reasonable, and nice. We do not recognize or acknowledge that in fact we are advocating, using the format of questions to present our case. The recipient of such an easing-in approach usually recognizes that she is being led or set up, and often responds by advocating for her position. Since we have not acknowledged (often even to ourselves) that we are advocating, her response appears defensive, resistant, and unreasonable to us. It can become a cycle of escalating frustration with little learning, until one party capitulates or one withdraws. That kind of inquiry is informed by Model I social virtues, and is to be avoided.

Advocacy is important for effective communication. To engage in fair and open conversation and decision-making, everyone must put his ideas and positions on the table. We are often hesitant to say clearly what we think or want. We have been taught that it is not polite to do so. In this, we were taught an error. It is rude to withhold our own ideas and positions when we have asked others to share theirs. It is unjust to ask others to put their thoughts out for people to evaluate while refusing to subject our own thoughts to the same process. It is devaluing of others to ask them to spend time sharing their ideas, when we are privately holding to our own ideas, which are undiscussable and not subject to influence. When we have developed advocacy skills, we will not find ourselves in situations like Gellerd's, in which people were being held responsible for ignoring thoughts she did not disclose and information she did not share. To behave justly, we must develop skill and comfort in advocacy. The most effective advocacy not only articulates our position clearly and offers the data we used to get there but also encourages the listener to inquire of us, asking for clarification or for data that are not present, and pointing out perceived gaps in our reasoning.

When you use advocacy in tandem with inquiry, you have maximized the likelihood that the information you need to make good decisions and design effective strategies will be available. Advocacy combined with inquiry creates a context for a dynamic relationship that includes mutual help,

support, and respect, thereby allowing each participant the ability to participate with integrity. Relationships as well as decisions will improve as the
mutual learning process enhances everyone who participates.

Outcome Frame: Know What You Want

It is very helpful in preparing for an interaction to identify the outcome you
are seeking. To the extent that you are clear about what you want to accomplish, you will be better able to know if you got there. We usually have
some kind of outcome in mind for every interaction, even those initiated by
others, and even the ones that are a surprise. Once the interaction begins,
we need to decide what we believe the conversation is about and what role
we want to play. That allows us to decide what to say. In ordinary situations
we do this so quickly it is almost out of consciousness. In higher-stress
situations we may be more aware of the internal dialogue that says, "Can
we just get through this without having him blow up?" or another such
thought. However, whether we have planned carefully in advance for a
meeting, or are pressed to respond on the spot, we have some idea of what
we want to come out of the encounter, what outcome we are going for.

To the degree that we can become aware of the outcomes we have
posited for ourselves, we are able to evaluate them to determine the social
virtues by which they are driven. We can ask ourselves, "Is this maintaining
unilateral control?" "Is this a unilateral protection of someone else?" "Am I
trying to win?" or "Am I consulting with those who have a stake in this?"

Designed Blindness and the Community of Inquiry

Designed blindness is not a tool for effectiveness. It is a barrier. It has been
included here because it is the dynamic that, more than any other, defies
correction when we act alone. Designed blindness is the reason that all of
the tools described above are best employed within the context of a community of inquiry. By definition, we cannot know those things that we have
designed to be outside our awareness. We need others to tell us when we
are not practicing what we preach. Were that not so, we would have
already made the necessary corrections and become perfect by now.
We need others to teach us about our errors. They can best do that in a

community that has developed safe and trusting relationships built on norms that honor people and their ability to learn. It may be a community of as few as two or as many as a large congregation, but it needs to be intentionally cultivated. Such a community is a paradigm of faithfulness, a way to illumine the image of God in the people of God.

The Continuous Learning Loop

The tools listed above will vary in their effectiveness, depending on their applicability in any given situation. Sometimes you will find that your old familiar ways of operating are working fine. At other times the situation will demand something different. The organizations and the professionals who are most successful are those who detect when change is necessary and respond accordingly. The continuous learning loop will allow for the constant monitoring and correction of your practice. It can help with single-loop learning about what works and what doesn't. The process becomes its most powerful when it is used to ask double-loop questions that expand the horizon and invite creativity.

Because we are working with a continuous loop, it doesn't really have a beginning. You can start anywhere. The easiest and most likely time to engage it is when you discover a problem. After encountering the problem and engaging in whatever other kinds of discovery you need to make, you come up with an invention that you think will address it. After you have invented your solution, you will attempt to produce it, putting it into practice. Remember, it is here that a significant number of undetected errors occur. Sometimes the behavior we produce is not the same as what we intended in our invention. We are usually unaware of the gap. This gap creates a challenge for the next phase, evaluation. We need to evaluate the outcome. However, the outcome may not reflect the effectiveness of the invention, if there was a difference between what we meant to do and what we actually did. A disappointing outcome may be the result of an inadequate invention, or it may reflect an error in producing it. We must be careful to determine where the error occurred—in defining the problem, inventing a solution, or producing the invention. Thus the evaluation process leads to new discoveries, which in turn call forth new inventions. The learning loop is its own perpetual-motion machine of the mind. It never needs to stop.

Action Science Axioms

In addition to the tools summarized above, we offer the following axioms, which provide handles to retrieve some of these skills and insights. They have not all been discussed in detail, but are implicit in the material. Making them explicit should help you to hold onto them.

1. Conversation is a component of action and is a core feature of who you are.
2. If all behavior is designed, and if unawareness is behavior, then unawareness must be designed. This unawareness leads to skilled incompetence.
3. Never give one member of a group private feedback, especially one in power. It often results in others thinking that you are in his or her pocket. It can disturb the group's trust that all issues are open and discussable. *Always give feedback to the whole group.*
4. The issue, when giving feedback, is not "Will they be defensive?" but "What will we do with their defensiveness?" (We do not have control over the other's behavior, only our own.)

The array of tools I have set before you is a powerful collection. I presented the package as a professional toolbox, each item chosen for the ways in which it can increase the effectiveness of your professional practice. There is no limit, however, on where you might use them. The tools it contains can be helpful in all areas of your life—intimate, social, personal, and organizational. I invite you to do so.

These tools do not stand alone. You already have a well-equipped cache of instruments and devices that have sustained you in your work. I want you to hold on to the tools you already have. The new ones are intended to enhance your repertoire and increase your skills at learning, so that your repertoire is elastic, always expanding to take in more. It will be easier if you share the tools with others in your community. Having a big common closet will keep the tools well-used, the linkages primed, and the sharpness maintained.

Striving with God and with Humans

> Jacob was left alone; and a man wrestled with him until daybreak.
> When the man saw that he did not prevail against Jacob, he struck
> him on the hip socket, and Jacob's hip was put out of joint as he
> wrestled with him. Then he said, "Let me go, for the day is break-
> ing." But Jacob said, "I will not let you go, unless you bless me."
> So he said to him, "What is your name?" And he said, "Jacob."
> Then the man said, "You shall no longer be called Jacob, but
> Israel, for you have striven with God and with humans, and have
> prevailed." Then Jacob asked him, "Please tell me your name."
> But he said, "Why is it that you ask my name?" And there he
> blessed him. So Jacob called the place Peniel, saying "For I have
> seen God face to face, and yet my life is preserved" [Gen.
> 32:24-30].

For many who have chosen the religious life, conflict is uncomfortable
and sometimes the object of disapproval and dismay. The assumptions of
this book have been very different. The tools I have given you and the
social virtues embraced assume that conflict will occur. Sometimes it is
necessary and to be encouraged.

The story of Jacob wrestling with the man/angel is reassuring. Jacob
does not flinch from the necessary conflict. He steps into it. Jacob and the
angel engage in extremely stressful and threatening conflict. Yet Jacob and
the man hold each other in high regard. They value the other's willingness
to stay in the engagement. The outcomes are telling.

While he is wrestling with the man, Jacob's hip is put out of joint. He is
changed. That change stays with him for life. He no longer walks like other
men, but with a limp, a reminder that he has striven with God and has
prevailed.

When we take up the difficult work of honest and respectful conflict,
we too will be changed. We may walk differently in the world from other
people. We may limp. It is hard work. But it is God's work. A little limp can
be a good thing, reminding us of our limitations, our less-than-perfect behavior, our attempts to grasp that which is beyond our reach. The limp may
be a sign that we have prevailed in our striving with God, but it remains also
as the reminder that God is God and we are not. It is the mark of humanity
and humility.

When Jacob took up wrestling with the man, hand to hand, leg to leg, cheek by jowl, he was surprised to discover that he had seen God. We too can see God when we allow ourselves to touch another with that kind of intensity and humility. The theme in Jacob's tale is repeated in the course of Hebrew and Christian Scripture. When we authentically encounter and engage another, God is revealed, and is with us.

The result of this frightening act for Jacob was a blessing. He was blessed *because* he had "striven with God and with humans, and [had] prevailed" (Gen. 32:28b). The man/angel interprets the outcome as prevailing. Notice that in the story the angel is not destroyed. Prevailing in this story meant not giving up, not relinquishing contact, not abdicating, but hanging in with the struggle. Prevailing meant that Jacob was preserved without having extinguished the angel. Prevailing meant that everyone was a winner.

Striving, engaging with God and with humans, hanging in with the struggle using all of one's faith, one's heart and one's might, when done with humility, integrity and deep respect for the other, yields blessings. So teaches the Scripture.

Dear reader, may you go forth then like Jacob. Wrestle with God and humans. Know the touch of humility. And may your encounter be holy, yielding blessings in your ministry for you and those whom you touch.

NOTES

Foreword

1. Chris Argyris, *Flawed Advice and the Management Trap* (New York: Oxford University Press, 2000).

Preface

1. Henry W. Bellows, "The Suspense of Faith," an address to the alumni of Harvard Divinity School, July 19, 1859 (Boston: C. S. Francis & Co. 1859) 35, 37.

Acknowledgments

1. Chris Argyris, *Theory and Practice: Increasing Professional Effectiveness* (San Francisco: Jossey Bass, 1974).

Chapter 2. Trapped by Virtue

1. This term was coined by Chris Argyris and Donald Schon.

2. Chris Argyris has taken his work, and his sample "X-Y" case, to every continent on the planet. Cross-culturally tested, these social virtues and the meanings that Model I attributes to them have been validated universally to the extent that such validation is possible. It is conceivable that some culture might test differently, but to this date, no such culture has been found.

3. In Deborah Tannen's work published in *You Just Don't Understand* (New York: Ballentine Books, 1991), she identifies gender differences in communication. These differences may compound the difficulty in discovering errors across gender lines. According to Tannen, when women tell stories about their difficulties, they are seeking connection, sympathy, and bonding. Men do not generally use stories about problems for these

relational purposes. Consequently, men hear these stories as requests to fix the problem, which they then try to do. Women become angry and frustrated in response. Capable of fixing their own problems, the women feel distanced by the men's response and diminished by the fixer's superior attitude. They were trying to bond. The men get angry, wondering why those women asked anyway, if they didn't want to know what to do. This gender gap contains echoes of the rabbi/sisterhood misunderstanding.

4. Rabbi Nachman of Breslov was born in Poland in 1772, the great grandson of the great Baal Shem Tov, founder of the Hasidic movement. The Hasidic tradition is one of mysticism and ecstasy, utilizing story and the oral tradition to inspire and instruct the people. This story has been told and retold by generations of rabbis and teachers. One version of it appears in *Rabbi Nachman's Stories*, Aryeh Kaplan, trans. (Jerusalem: Breslov Research Institute, 1983).

5. Adapted from Chris Argyris, *Reasoning, Learning and Action: Individual and Organizational* (San Francisco: Jossey-Bass, 1982), 87. (This book is out of print.)

6. Adapted from Argyris, *Reasoning, Learning and Action.*

Chapter 4. Coaching for Change
1. We are drawing from the communications and change schema developed within neurolinguistic programming.

2. Robert Kegan, *In Over Our Heads: The Mental Demands of Modern Life* (Cambridge: Harvard University Press, 1996), 288.

3. Richard Powers, "Eyes Wide Open," *New York Times Magazine*, April 18, 1999, 81.

Chapter 5. Constructing Your Own Case
1. My work is an extension of the work by Chris Argyris and his associates, who developed the discipline of action science. I use their model of case presentation as our foundation, to which I have added. Therefore, I have retained their language of "right-hand column" and "left-hand column" because in the action science literature they are technical terms having specific meanings. When I repeatedly encountered an internal dialogue with a deeper structure, I chose to call it the "left-of-the-left-hand column" to maintain consistency with the action science terminology.

Chapter 6. A Community of Learning

1. Peter L. Steinke, "When Congregations Are Stuck," *Christian Century*, April 7, 1999, 387.

2. Ronald C. Arnett, *Communication and Community: Implications of Martin Buber's Dialogue* (Carbondale: Southern Illinois Press, 1986), 99.

Chapter 7. From Community Spirit to Spiritual Community

1. Paul Tillich, *The Courage to Be* (New Haven: Yale University Press, 1952), chapters 4 and 5.

2. Martin Buber, *On Judaism* (New York: Schocken Books, 1967), 212.

3. Elie Wiesel, *The Gates of the Forest* (New York: Schocken Books, 1982).

4. Contemporary oral tradition.

5. We are not dealing here with the whole phenomenology of human sin. I am convinced, however, that the constraints on thinking, reasoning, and action that are imposed by a Model I framework necessarily and inevitably produce sin. Without the options of Model II as a counterpart and corrective, the Model I world by itself is sinful. Moving toward Model II involves a kind of sanctification, reconciliation, or growth in grace.

6. Argyris, *Reasoning, Learning and Action*, xi.

7. John Bunyan, *The Pilgrim's Progress* (New York: New American Library, 1981), 1.

8. Bunyan, *Pilgrim's Progress*, 18.

9. Bunyan, *Pilgrim's Progress*, 18.

10. Argyris, *Reasoning, Learning and Action*, 469-70.

11. Bunyan, *Pilgrim's Progress*, 19.

12. Bunyan, *Pilgrim's Progress*, 22-23.